Praise for *Your Meaning Legacy*

"We believe, as Laura does, that we are all on this earth to make a difference. No matter your age or stage of life, *Your Meaning Legacy* will prepare you to share your life and learnings with generations to come. Read it and mark your place in time."

— KEN AND MARGIE BLANCHARD, cofounders of The Ken Blanchard Companies and coauthors of *Servant Leadership in Action*

"If you care about your impact on the world and your family, read *Your Meaning Legacy*. It will teach you how to pass on what's most important."

— KEVIN CASHMAN, Global Head of CEO & Executive Development, Korn Ferry, Best-Selling Author of *Leadership from the Inside Out* and *The Pause Principle*

"This wonderful, meaningful and important work encourages, educates and dares the reader to touch their heart's needs and to be present and mindful to their true mission. *Your Meaning Legacy* fills a vast void and is a must read."

— MICHAEL F. KAY, Author of *The Feel Rich Project*

"Laura Roser openly shares her passion and a much-needed process that helps readers pass on the legacy they want instead of leaving it to chance."

— CHARLIE DOUGLAS, Chairman, Multidisciplinary Committee, National Association of Estate Planners & Councils

"Laura captures the power of philanthropy in this truly meaningful book."

— BILL LITTLEJOHN, CEO and Senior Vice President, Sharp HealthCare Foundation

"Laura has distilled a meaningful way to outline the essential framework to take a theoretical ideal and build something concrete and lasting that can impact your family and the community. The book provides a thorough understanding on ways to capture your legacy and involve those you love in the process. A great read!"

— MICHAEL G. STUART, JD, CPA, Co-Founder of The Family Legacy Alliance

"This masterfully crafted primer on 'legacy' should be required reading for those individuals and families who seek to amplify their impact now and for generations to come. As a fellow pioneer in 'more than money' legacy and wealth management, I am glad to report that Laura has set out a path that is worthy of following. Your journey should begin by reading these pages."

— MONROE "ROEY" DIEFENDORF, JR., Author of *3 Dimensional Wealth: A Radically Sane Perspective On Wealth Management* and *A Better Way: Using Purposeful Trusts To Preserve Values & Valuables In Perpetuity*

"Use this valuable guide to learn how to share what is important to you, how you felt along the way, and how you want your wisdom transferred—and do it all in a fun, meaningful, and lasting way."

— FLORA MORRIS BROWN, PH.D., Author of *Color Your Life Happy: Create Your Unique Path and Claim the Joy You Deserve*

GOLDEN LEGACY
—— PRESS ——

YOUR
MEANING
LEGACY

How to Cultivate & Pass On
Non-Financial Assets

LAURA A. ROSER

GOLDEN LEGACY PRESS
Solona Beach, CA

GOLDEN LEGACY
——— PRESS ———
249 HWY 101, Ste 524
Solana Beach, CA 92075

First Golden Legacy Press paperback edition April 2018

Manufactured in the United States of America

10 9 8 7 6 5 4 3 2 1

Library of Congress Cataloging-in-Publication Data is available.

ISBN 978-0-9997792-1-7 (hardcover)
ISBN 978-0-9997792-0-0 (paperback)
ISBN 978-0-9997792-2-4 (ebook)

For additional Meaning Legacy™ planning resources, please visit

www.meaninglegacytools.com

(Don't worry, no registration or password is required.)

To my future heirs.
I pray I won't mess you up too badly and that
I might even do a little good.

Contents

PART 3: CASE STUDIES

The Best Parts of Yourself
What Matters to You?

"The great use of life is to spend it for something that will outlast it."
—William James, American philosopher and psychologist

Estate planning traditionally focuses on your financial assets. But there's more to you than your physical wealth. What about your wisdom, beliefs, values, important family traditions, and stories? What about passing on crucial knowledge about your business, money management, or other skills?

Oftentimes, people don't think about the intangibles they should pass on to their heirs. Because estate planning is so wrapped up in transferring financial assets, figuring out how to pass on your real estate, investments, and collectibles becomes the goal. Once your financial team hands you your estate plan, you think you've got all your bases covered: You've got life insurance, a trust to avoid probate, an appointed executor, and so on.

Financial structuring, however, is only a piece of the puzzle. Your legacy extends far beyond the material possessions you have managed to accumulate.

I first started thinking about my legacy several years ago after a meeting with a financial advisor who initially hooked me with the sentence, "We have a process to help you pass on wisdom and principles to your kids." He then placed a sheet of paper in front of me that instructed me to list my values.

"Is there more?" I asked, holding up the paper. "I thought you said you had a process to pass on wisdom."

Instead of delving deeper into what I'd hoped would be a discussion about passing on meaningful knowledge to my loved ones, he began to pitch a whole life insurance policy that could be set up to align with my values. This is not what I wanted to hear.

Although I didn't act immediately, this experience planted a seed. At the time, I was running a marketing company and a real estate investment firm and hadn't prioritized my legacy. But things evolved. I experienced the highs and lows of the real estate market, the ups and downs of marriage, financial successes, and colossal personal and financial disaster.

By the time I reached the age of 31, I had gone from nothing to making millions, been in intense legal battles, lost all my financial assets, and discovered some significant blind spots in my marriage. I was left with debt, a group of wonderfully supportive friends and family, and a bed with a 600-thread-count duvet cover from my previous life. Everything else was gone: no more big house on the hill, no more sleek BMW, no more 5-star vacations, no more Amex card, no more husband.

At this point, I began thinking deeply about what my life represented, along with the thought of writing a memoir. I'd experienced extreme success and extreme failure. But what was all my striving for? This existential crisis prompted me to delve into a comprehensive examination of legacy. After years of focusing on building up financial assets that had all disappeared in a period of two years—along with my marriage and the dreams my husband and I had shared—I began to consider what was truly important to me. Then, a stifling realization hit me: If my plans hadn't been derailed, I very well may have spent my whole life focusing on acquiring more stuff, living to please others, using work as an excuse to avoid introspection—all with little fulfillment for myself.

Thankfully, life had other plans. I rediscovered what I intrinsically knew all those years ago when I sat in front of that whole life insurance salesman. Focusing only on financial assets and pretending that a simple sheet of swell values somehow gives life meaning is silly. That's not a legacy I'd be proud to pass on. Even though I knew I was missing something, I wasn't sure how to articulate what I wanted to pass on or how to do it. So I set out to determine what makes a meaningful legacy.

In the spirit of Napoleon Hill—the man who studied over 500 self-made millionaires to learn the secrets of their success—I went on a quest to interview the best and brightest in legacy development. Since then, I've talked with many estate planning attorneys, financial planners, personal historians, anthropologists, religious leaders, family counselors, and life coaches. I've studied everything I could get my hands on about character development, legacy planning, storytelling, spirituality, philosophy, happiness, effectively giving through charitable contributions, and successful family systems. My team and I have interviewed some of the most accomplished people in the world—business executives, millionaires, celebrities, best-selling authors, philanthropic leaders, artists, and scientists—and we discovered that accomplishing great things doesn't mean you'll have a great legacy. Without the proper system and focus, your legacy will be accidental.

Throughout this process, I concluded that no company had exactly what I was after all those years ago. There were bits and pieces of advice, ideas about writing ethical wills, fun tips about collecting family memories, and trust structures to ensure an heir's compliance, but no fully realized system of creating the kind of personal legacy I wanted to leave behind.

Before my focus on legacy, I spent over a decade running an integrated marketing services firm that packaged up companies to attract investment capital, launch an IPO, or introduce new concepts to potential customers. I learned that managing your legacy is a similar process. Businesses don't attract interest based on fundamentals alone; there must be a story, an educational process, and an emotional hook that reveals the vision and connects with a universal desire for a better future. Your legacy is made great for the same reason: It emotionally and competently connects with the people you care about to inspire them.

There are several motivations behind creating a meaningful legacy. Some of the most-mentioned benefits are:

- More fulfillment and purpose in your life.

- A closer family who enjoys improved communication and joint goals.

- Children exhibiting higher levels of self-esteem, loyalty to the family, independence, and a solid foundation of morals and principles to live by.

- No regrets—you will not reach the end of your life and wonder why you didn't express your love before it was too late.

- Greater peace of mind knowing that your children and loved ones have an "instruction manual" from you outlining lessons you've learned, what you believe in, and how you have done practical things (such as manage money or grow your business).

- Building a legacy to be remembered for, providing hope, a sense of pride, and inspiration for future generations.

- Creating a tangible record of your life that will be treasured and not fade over time, as memories tend to do.

- Leveraging your impact on the community in supporting a cause you care about.

Financial legacy planning covers a variety of topics, from financial structuring to business succession planning to tax implications. There are many great books to read and experts to follow in these areas. At my company, we work with these experts according to our clients' needs.

But this book isn't about giving you the best ways to set up your family foundation or avoid probate; it's about the "soul" of legacy planning. It's what branding is to business. It is the heart of your legacy plan—the often-overlooked but most important aspect of truly capturing your essence as a person and furthering your vision for the future. This type of focus is what we call a Meaning Legacy™.

A Meaning Legacy typically affects two types of audiences:

1. Your community, or the public.

2. Your family and loved ones.

You'll need to treat these audiences differently because the kind of information you share with each is significantly different. Your children, for example, will have a different concept of you than will the people who've just read an article about you in the *Wall Street Journal* highlighting your new charity.

The public side of your legacy has much more of a corporate feel—branding you as if you were running for political office. It's all about marketing you as a great man or woman with a mission for good. I've heard pushback on this concept—the idea that it's narcissistic or egotistical—and some of those elements may manifest at times, but truly, you are here to make a difference.

In his 2011 book *Start Something that Matters*, Blake Mycoskie, founder of Tom's Shoes—the corporation that gives away a pair of shoes to someone in need with each purchase—writes about the power of his story. It finally hit him how important he was to the equation when he ran into a woman wearing his shoes. Not knowing who he was, she told his story to him, along with the many amazing things he was doing with the company. It was only after she'd gushed about how incredible he was that he revealed his identity. She'd had no idea; she'd just thought he was some stranger asking about her shoes. This story has about ten times more impact than if Mycoskie had simply written, "We provide people with shoes."

The private side of your legacy is about connection with loved ones. Traditionally, this is your family. When the term "family" is used throughout this book, it could mean your friends, business partners, nieces and nephews, or employees. You don't need to have children to pass on a legacy; all you need is people you care about.

You want to give your heirs the greatest advantages, and your wisdom, love and family heritage is a significant component. If you have not shared the most important parts of you—your dreams, your journey, your struggles, your successes, your beliefs—with your loved ones, you have not fulfilled your potential.

This book shows you how to define, construct, and implement a meaningful legacy. It covers a comprehensive step-by-step process. I have synthesized my team's research and our years of experience in a variety of disciplines, from family dynamics to systems design to video production to publishing.

This book is broken into three parts:

- Part 1: Legacy Foundation Principles

- Part 2: Components of a Meaning Legacy

- Part 3: Case Studies

Meant to be an introduction to planning your Meaning Legacy, this book is best read from beginning to end. You may skip the parts that don't apply to you—if you don't have children, for instance, you may not be interested in creating a family mission statement. There are a variety of topics I include simply because I want to give you a holistic view of the entire scope of a Meaning Legacy plan. Individual components could each be a book of their own.

The study of legacy has become my obsession, not only to improve my own life but also to provide a resource for others. This book is for everyone, regardless of monetary wealth, who wishes to live a meaningful life. As Eleanor Roosevelt wrote, "If people come up the financial ladder but still maintain a low educational standard, with its lack of appreciation of many of the things of artistic and spiritual value, the nation will not be able to grow to its real stature." Thus, the audience for this book is not defined by its economic standing but instead by its ideology. Developing a great legacy is within the grasp of anyone with a clear vision.

I believe you have something important to contribute to the world. Whether it's as meaningful as creating a close, resilient family or as big as pledging to eradicate world hunger, each one of us is meant to do something great and pass it on. This book will show you how.

PART 1

LEGACY FOUNDATION
PRINCIPLES

1

The Meaning Legacy
Assets of Excellence

"It is up to us to live up to the legacy that was left for us, and to leave a legacy that is worthy of our children and of future generations."

—Christine Gregoire, American politician and attorney

Your assets can be broken into three main categories:

- *Character Assets*: Your meaningful relationships, values, health, spirituality, heritage, purpose, life experiences, talents, and plans for giving.

- *Intellectual Assets*: Your business systems, alliances, ideas, skills, traditions, reputation, and wisdom.

- *Financial Assets*: Your physical wealth, investments, and possessions.

Financial assets are passed along through proper structuring—such as a trust, or a foundation—ranging from the simple to the complex, depending on your level of affluence and tax reduction or estate planning goals. But rarely are your character and intellectual assets taken into account. Often, these assets are lost simply because there is not a structured way to identify them and pass them along to loved ones.

Why Wealth Transfer Fails 70 Percent of the Time

The old proverb "Shirtsleeves to shirtsleeves in three generations" is an accurate description of the cycle most wealthy families experience. One of the best examples of this is what happened with the fortune of Cornelius Vanderbilt, the second-richest person in American history.[1] At his death in 1877, he left $105 million, 95 percent of which went to one son, William Henry Vanderbilt. Adjusted for inflation, that's equivalent to approximately $200 billion today. Although William doubled his father's fortune to over $200 million, William's children and grandchildren squandered the money on mansions, yachts, and thoroughbred horses.[2]

According to one study that surveyed 3,250 wealthy families, when wealth is transferred to an heir, 70 percent of the time, it is lost due to mismanagement, poor investment choices, and other mistakes.[3] In the book *Preparing Heirs: Five Steps to Successful Transition of Family Wealth and Values*, Roy Williams and Vic Preisser cite three reasons wealth transfers result in so many catastrophes:

- 15 percent of failed wealth transfers are a result of taxes,

---

1 According to a CNN Money article written by Steve Hargreaves entitled "Squandering the Family Fortune: Why Rich Families Are Losing Money," published on June 25, 2014.

2 According to a Forbes article written by Natalie Robehmed titled "The Vanderbilts: How American Royalty Lost Their Crown Jewels," published on July 14, 2014.

3 According to Roy Williams and Vic Preisser, authors of *Preparing Heirs: Five Steps to Successful Transition of Family Wealth and Values*, and studies done by the *Economist* and the Massachusetts Institute of Technology.

legal issues, and poor financial planning.

- 25 percent of wealth transfers fail because of inadequately prepared heirs.

- 60 percent of wealth transfers fail because of breakdowns in communication and trust within the family.

In other words, 85 percent of failed wealth transfers are a direct result of not properly passing on intellectual and character assets, and some of the remaining 15 percent could be solved by transferring those assets as well.

The question then becomes, how do you successfully pass on these softer assets? And, more importantly, how do you do it in a way that leads to happiness? According to the book *Fortune's Children: The Fall of the House of Vanderbilt*, Willy Vanderbilt, grandson of Cornelius, remarked, "My life was never destined to be quite happy. It was laid out along lines which I could not foresee, almost from earliest childhood. It has left me with nothing to hope for, with nothing definite to seek or strive for. Inherited wealth is a real handicap to happiness." One can't help but wonder if this lack of hope led to the demise of the family's estate.

Fortunately, not all heirs feel this sense of hopelessness, but it is the danger of not properly establishing a family belief system built around meaning. If a family's purpose is to create heirs who are happy, grateful, and competent, wealth can enhance the journey to a more self-actualized life. If, however, this process is not managed, entropy can take over, and may change the family in unpredictable ways, which typically means the wealth either causes harm to its heirs or doesn't create the benefits it was intended for. Studies have shown, for example, that affluent families have a higher proportion of teens who suffer from substance abuse issues, depression, and anxiety in comparison to middle-class or even low-income teenagers.[4]

Without the emotional tools to cope with their good fortune, many children may experience feelings of inferiority. Consider this excerpt from the book *Rich Kids* by John Sedgwick, who interviewed 75 heirs about the effects of their inheritance:

> For all rich kids, the act of inheritance is entirely passive. Yet this sometimes makes the guilt more severe, and more permanent. True criminals, at least, have something to confess. They can receive forgiveness, they can reform, they can put the sins behind them. But rich kids start to feel they are the sin themselves, and every crime that was ever committed hangs on their heads. They see the inequity that lies about them, or read about it in their money mail, and they think they are responsible for it. Because they are on top, they must be squashing those on the bottom. This is the true embarrassment of riches.

Creators of wealth may have difficulty relating to this kind of thinking because they didn't grow up in circumstances similar to what their kids or grandkids experience. The majority of wealth in the United States is self-made,[5] which means most wealthy individuals came from middle-class or blue-collar backgrounds with their associated values. If your children do not come from the same economic circumstances as you did, you must consider what they're experiencing and take steps to help the entire family adapt to a new reality.

---

4 Suniya S. Luthar, "The Culture of Affluence: Psychological Costs of Material Wealth," *Child Development* 74, no. 6 (2003).

5 A 2017 study by BMO Private Bank found that 67 percent of high-net worth Americans are self-made millionaires. Only 8 percent inherited their wealth.

I've attended conferences devoted specifically to the problem of failed wealth transfer, and interviewed financial experts and affluent families about their experiences. Some best practices certainly have emerged and some families are doing well into their sixth and seventh generations, but the truth is there is no way to ensure that wealth will last for generations. The success of the fortune depends upon the family itself and favorable circumstances. Growing the family fortune and encouraging each member's personal progression is like gardening. You can plant a garden and care for it using every best practice, but anything from bad weather to insects may ruin it all. Still, without the hard work, you'd have nothing; and so it is with family wealth.

An affluent family is a complicated system and many tools are needed to tend that particular garden. You need competent advisors, attorneys, and management; the right structuring; professionals to assist with mental and emotional health as problems arise; and experts to help with specified tasks such as brokering a real estate transaction or representing the family in a lawsuit. These experts and key family members, however, must be guided by a common vision for a family to experience continuity across generations.

A Meaning Legacy provides direction for a family's progression through life and a structure by which to pass on its philosophical vision. The most important part is not the vision itself; it's the process of uncovering and sculpting that vision as you go along. This process enables family members to trust each other, work together for the common good of the family, cultivate open dialogue, create responsible children with their own visions, and know they can adapt when hardship befalls them.

Beyond Financial Success

In their book *Just Enough*, authors Laura Nash and Howard Stevenson write about their findings which revealed that many top executives are successful monetarily but often feel they are lacking in relationships, family connection, work-life balance, and character development.

Their study came up with four metrics that matter most in creating a meaningful life:

1. Happiness: Experiencing pleasure or contentment in and about your life.

2. Achievement: Accomplishing goals that compare favorably to others who have strived for something similar.

3. Significance: Positively impacting the people you care about.

4. Legacy: Using your knowledge, values, and accomplishments as a way to help others with their future success.

When you develop each of these metrics, the authors found, life takes on a heightened sense of purpose. In the coming chapters, we will focus heavily on how to enhance the significance and legacy metrics in your life.

What Is a Meaning Legacy?

A Meaning Legacy is the most valuable asset you can leave behind for your loved ones. Simply put, a Meaning Legacy preserves your life, lessons you've learned along your journey, and your vision for the future as a gift to those you care about. It's not only about leaving behind something great after you've died. It's about living life in a way that will positively impact those you love right here, right now.

To have the greatest effect, a Meaning Legacy should be accompanied by a solid financial strategy. Separating your family's philosophical vision from your financial structuring may make sense for some family members not involved with your finances, but for those who are privy to financial decisions, your family dynamics, values, and communication play significant roles in how the family fortune is managed and in your heirs' financial competence. I strongly suggest involving your wealth advisory team in creating governance processes based on personal and family principles you define as a part of your legacy vision.

The Seven Components of a Meaning Legacy

You have worked hard to build a successful life. Your money, home, and possessions are a manifestation of a mindset you have spent years cultivating. That mindset, the lessons you've learned, the experiences you've had, and the love you've shared? Those are what impact your family and what your children will treasure. They can also add up to become an instruction manual of sorts when your children or loved ones need a little extra help.

An effective Meaning Legacy comprises seven main components:

1. Beliefs, Values, and Vision

2. Master Stories

3. Experiential Bonds

4. Family Heritage

5. Community Impact

6. Systems for Living

7. Public Presence

See Figure 1 for a graphical representation. We'll briefly review each of these components before we move on to the next chapters.

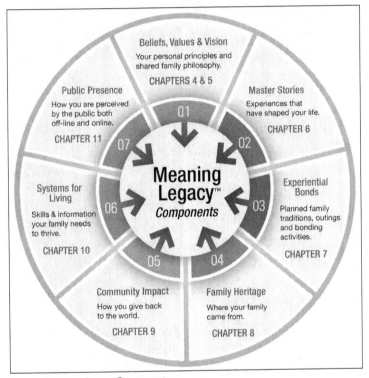

Figure 1. Meaning Legacy Components

Component 1:

Beliefs, Values, and Vision

A belief system is made powerful by those who believe in it and agree to abide by its principles. A dollar has value because you and I—and billions of others—have agreed that a piece of paper with George Washington's face on it represents something. The Declaration of Independence, capitalism, democracy, or Christianity are highly powerful ideologies that shape the decisions and desires of millions of people.

In his book *Sapiens: A Brief History of Humankind*, Yuval Noah Harari writes about the difference between objective, subjective, and inter-subjective phenomena.

An objective phenomenon is independent of our consciousness or beliefs. I, for instance, don't have to believe in or know about gravity in order for it to exist. If I walk off a cliff, I'll still fall to the ground, despite my ignorance. This is true now and was true before gravity was named or discovered.

A subjective phenomenon depends upon the beliefs of a single individual and changes or evolves as that person changes his or her mind. So if I believe that I manifest wealth by holding a blue rock in my hand, but then my friend laughs at me and I decide it's not true, when that belief changes, it only affects me because no one else had the same belief.

An inter-subjective phenomenon is when an entire community shares the same subjective beliefs. If someone within the believing community changes her belief or dies, it doesn't matter—there are enough believers to sustain the ideology. When someone denounces capitalism, for example, it has very little effect on that ideology because there are millions of supporters. But if the pool of believers is weak, a change made by a small number of individuals threatens the whole system. If someone invents a religion that believes donkeys are the great creators of the universe and they recruit ten people as followers, and then half of them die in a tragic car accident on the way to church, and then the other half decide this is all a little too kooky for them, the religion ends.

Your family is an inter-subjective system. You have joint beliefs and principles that guide your decisions. If you do not share your individual beliefs with your family or document them, they die with you. The key is to create a strong joint ideology that isn't completely lost if one person stops believing or someone dies. Of course, you want to give your family members freedom to express themselves and adapt, but the clearer you are about a joint family vision, the more likely your family will be able to survive from generation to generation with a strong set of principles enabling them to work together, foster loyalty, learn, grow, and thrive.

It doesn't make sense to reinvent the wheel every time key members in the family pass away—especially if you've managed to create a life of abundance and beauty. Without the proper systems to pass on your ideology, your family is left in the Dark Ages, trying to make advancements when crucial knowledge has been lost.

The first step is identifying what you believe; this process is outlined in detail in Chapter 4. In Chapter 5, we cover how to create a joint belief system with your family.

Component 2:

Master Stories

Some experiences affect you more than others do. These are what Jewish theologian Michael Goldberg[6] has termed "master stories." Master stories transform and shape who you are and form the way you think about the world. Everyone has different master stories depending on the events of their lives and how they processed them.

Master stories can be negative or positive, depending on the teller's interpretation of events. For example, I know someone who didn't discover he was adopted until his early twenties, when a woman he knew as a child accidentally told him. When he confronted his parents, his mother began sobbing and his father ignored him. Because of the shame he felt and the lack of a family dialogue, this story led to years of psychological harm.

Master stories can also be positive, such as tales of triumph, courage, and success, like the first time you realized you were good at baseball or how your favorite teacher positively influenced your life.

At a rudimentary level, most advice seems cliché: "Follow the golden rule"; "Work hard, play hard"; "Believe in yourself"; "Always tell the truth." What forges a deeper connection with your audience is sharing how you felt during an experience. This is how wisdom is transferred.

A thousand people can say they value honesty, but each one will have a different concept of what "honesty" means.

---

6 Michael Goldberg, author of *Jews and Christians: Getting Our Stories Straight*.

When we tell stories, it reveals who we are and what we represent much better than a list of condensed principles does.

I once asked my mother if she had any stories of courageous moments. She said:

> When I was in grade school, I had a teacher who accused me and two other girls of cheating. But I knew I didn't cheat. I would never cheat. My parents taught me cheating was one of the worst things you could do. The other girls started crying, but I refused to cry. I was furious; there was no way I'd give him the satisfaction. I told him he was wrong, crossed my arms, and looked at him defiantly. Finally, he said, 'Well, obviously, you didn't cheat. You can go.'

This story goes beyond the cliché of "Stand up for what you believe in" and transforms it from an abstract principle into a concrete experience that allows the listener to extract wisdom and apply it to their unique situation. That's what good stories do.

Usually, there is some form of conflict in a master story. As Wilma Rudolph said, "Triumph can't be had without struggle." Overcoming your struggles can be the most character-shaping experiences of your life as well as teach your family about resilience.

In Chapter 6, we will cover how to unearth your master stories, what stories are crucial to pass on to your children, and how you can determine what should be shared.

Component 3:

Experiential Bonds

Experiential bonds are significant one-time events or repeated experiences that are remembered with fondness, such as going to your special family spot every summer and performing the same traditions. It's about creating quality time that prioritizes increasing love and then creating an environment for wisdom transfer.

Sometimes it's hard to know when or how to interact with your family in a meaningful way. Are you going to sit your kids in the corner and drone on for three hours while they distractedly look at their smartphones? Will they be receptive? Maybe they aren't yet ready for your wisdom; maybe you don't know how to share it in an inspirational way.

In Chapter 7, we cover how you can create meaningful experiences and teaching topics for your family, and convey them in a way that is fun, not burdensome. These experiences, such as family vacations, outings, and even dinners, should not be planned and scheduled until the life is sucked out of them. Fun should take priority and may take the form of having competitions as a family, talking about new ideas and dreams, or learning new things together. You are trying to cultivate experiences that will last, not just be remembered for the quality of the hotels or restaurants that you visited. You want experiences that will impact your children's way of thinking. One way to do this is through gamification—creating challenges or games for family events. Another way is through traditions or family projects, not to mention storytelling and passing along the family's master stories.

We've found that the most successful families plan at least

one large event per year and several smaller events throughout the year. One exceptionally close family—the patriarch runs a multibillion-dollar aerospace company in Florida with his two sons—has family dinners every Sunday. "Some people go to church on Sundays," the father told me, "but we meet for dinners as a family with my two sons, their wives, and my grandchildren. If we receive an invite for something else on Sunday, we always decline. Time with our family is sacred."

Component 4:

Family Heritage

There's no question that documenting your family's biological roots gives you an anchor, establishing your identity and helping you to understand what family behaviors you can build upon or learn from. In fact, studies conducted at Emory University[7] have shown that kids who know about their family's past are more empathetic, have better coping skills, and have higher self-esteem.

There are ways to document and archive family history that can be fun and engage your entire family. Doing this correctly, however, can be a little tricky; too much inconsequential information can dilute your message.

Determining the important events and milestones often takes hindsight. Or, as Joseph Campbell said, ". . .when you reach an advanced age and look back over your lifetime, it can seem to have had a consistent order and plan, as though com-

---

7 Jennifer G. Bohanek, et al. "Family Narrative Interaction and Children's Sense of Self," *Family Process* 45, no. 1 (March 2006): 39–54.

posed by some novelist. Events that when they occurred had seemed accidental and of little moment turn out to have been indispensable factors in the composition of a consistent plot."

Learning which aspects to highlight and focus on is the difference between a family heritage of minutia and one of greatness. In Chapter 8, we will review what to focus on. Avoiding irrelevant information and highlighting the gems in your past will provide you and your heirs with a sense of purpose and place.

Consider how meaningful it would be, for example, for your grandchildren to learn that the family business was started by their great-grandfather who immigrated from Ireland with nothing more than two dollars in his pocket and his mother's recipe for soup. Just one story like this can change the way your heirs view the family business and, in turn, handle it in the future.

Component 5:

Community Impact

I used to send money to a variety of causes without thinking much about it or getting involved. I'd get a mailer from Smile Train and send them some money. Someone at the grocery store would ask me to donate to clean energy initiatives, and I would. My friend would invite me to a fundraiser to save rain forests in South America, and I'd write a check. There's nothing wrong with giving to any of these causes, but I've learned that this shoot-from-the-hip approach has very little positive effect in comparison to aligning with a cause that truly turns you on. And I'm not alone; my experience tracks with the many philanthropists, impact investors, and community leaders I've interviewed. The more deeply they care about a cause they support, the more it becomes a part of who they are.

Philanthropy is one of the best ways to teach humility, gratitude, and responsibility. But writing a check to a charity in and of itself is not going to create a meaningful experience. Just like finding the right calling (rather than only working for a wage) produces passion and vigor, identifying your giving personality and taking steps to contribute in ways that resonate with your core can dramatically raise your sense of purpose. CBS ran a story of a man named Eugene Yoon who saw a video about a man who was paralyzed and couldn't walk. Eugene decided to quit his job and go on an extensive hike to raise $80,000 for this man so that he could get an apparatus that would help him walk again. Along his journey, Yoon posted videos on YouTube and asked for donations. He reached his monetary goal long before he finished his hike. Eugene was just one man with essentially no money but a very real vision. You may not be in a position to dramatically alter your life to help a stranger the way Eugene did, but when you think about your impact on the world, it should inspire you.

There are limitless ways to serve, but only a handful will fit with your personality. We've identified seven giving personality types and a system for meaningfully incorporating philanthropy into your life and the lives of your children. In Chapter 9, we'll review how to add a giving component to your legacy.

Component 6:

Systems for Living

Your family is a living organism. Your purpose is to help it grow and evolve by becoming closer, healthier, more capable, and loving.

Systems for Living refers to systems you've put in place to ensure a productive family, fulfilling personal life, and legacy of significance. A part of documenting your Systems for Living has to do with building your "team," or family. Chapter 10 outlines processes for creating measurable progress with your personal legacy and encouraging your family to work and live together well. An example of this is holding weekly family meetings. Just twenty minutes per week could make a huge impact on your family. People who have done this with their children have reported significantly better communication and family participation after just a couple weeks. In that chapter, we also review the fundamentals of developing a Family Brain Trust, which will serve as the structure by which you capture and archive important information.

While the United States is a highly "me-focused" country, working together with your family for the benefit of the entire group helps your children develop an "us-focused" orientation. Cultivating an ability to care for and cooperate with others is a skill your children can apply to running their own families or businesses. Life has a lot of ups and downs, and a strong support system—whether through friends or family—is essential.

Money management and interacting with advisors is important here, too. Many parents don't want to worry their children with finances. This is a mistake—your kids will grow up not knowing how to function financially. They won't learn these skills on their own early on and certainly not at the level of sophistication you have developed. Financial systems can start small and improve over time so when your kids want to build a business or make a big investment, it won't be a pipe dream—they'll have the skills and competence to pull it off.

Component 7:

Public Presence

Your public presence is how you are viewed by the world. It includes your personal reputation (both online and off-line), media coverage, and your public message (in the form of books, websites, blogs, or videos). Although it can tie in with your company, your public legacy is not necessarily linked to your business. It is more about how you are perceived as an individual, philanthropist, or leader.

Everyone has a public-sharing comfort level. Some want to be in the spotlight, while others avoid it. Many wealthy people are especially sensitive to privacy issues. "It's better to fly under the radar," they reason. And to a large extent, it's a wise choice. It's easy to become a target if you announce to the world how wealthy you are, especially in a litigious society where the average business is sued every seven years and regulators like to hammer down nails that stick up. Not to mention the fear of attracting competitors to your business: If you start telling everyone you're making millions on collecting and selling old tires, you may see a decline in profits the next year as your business idea is imitated.

Despite all these pitfalls, your public presence matters—a lot. Here's why.

Privacy is disappearing. Either you manage your presence or others determine it for you. A bad reputation online can lead to lost deals, lost relationships, embarrassment, and, in extreme circumstances, being labeled the scapegoat in a criminal investigation.

A great online presence, on the other hand, can lead to superior deal flow, social support of your endeavors, and more fulfillment as you pass on a philosophical, community, or business legacy to better the world. This doesn't mean you should share everything about your private life. But when you control your own story, you are not at the mercy of fickle media, an upset employee who libels you online, or an ex who posts pictures of you drunk all over the internet. Having a clear plan to positively build your reputation and deal with potential catastrophe is a must.

Whether you're the face of your public legacy or it's your organization, you can structure your presence to reap the benefits of a good reputation. In Chapter 11, we will discuss the basics of a public legacy plan and what questions to consider.

Roadmap to Your Legacy

The next chapters cover obstacles, timing considerations, and the stages of legacy maturity you can expect to go through as you develop and implement your plan. Chapters 4 through 11 delve into each of the components of a Meaning Legacy, and Chapter 12 gives guidance about how to immortalize and share your legacy through the creation of legacy vehicles. Finally, in Part 3: Case Studies, we look at four examples of individuals at different life stages and how they accomplished their legacy objectives using our methods.

Figure 2 is an overall representation of what the legacy planning and implementation process entails. In order for your legacy to be most effective, you must craft each of the seven components of a Meaning Legacy in a way that clearly communicates your message to the outside world. Simply knowing your values or family stories isn't enough. These important parts of yourself must be presented and passed along in the right way for your loved ones to receive the optimum benefits. This book will take you through the entire process.

By the time you finish reading this book, you may reconsider how important your presence is to others.

Visit **www.meaninglegacytools.com** *for Meaning Legacy planning resources, including an outline of the planning process, a detailed legacy assessment, and other valuable information.*

Don't worry; we do not require you to register or enter your email to access these resources.

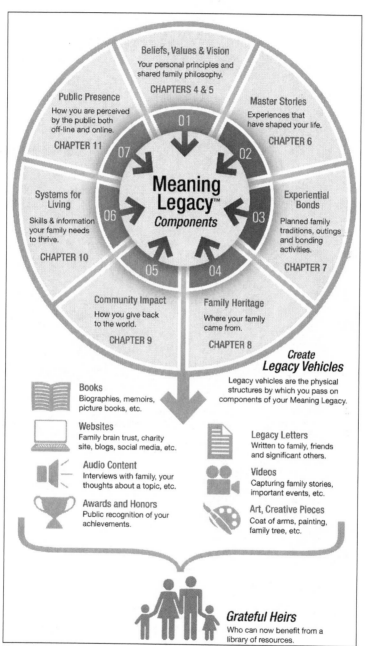

Figure 2. Meaning Legacy Planning Process

2

Before You Begin
Road Obstacles and Hazards

"Obstacles are those frightful things you see when you take your eyes off your goal."
—Henry Ford, American business magnate

Your legacy is made great by your positive effect on others and the joint vision you create together. On paper, this sounds great—who doesn't want to contribute positively to the lives of others? But in practice, it can get messy.

This doesn't mean a great legacy is not worth pursuing. There are, however, some obstacles to be aware of.

Mind Control Doesn't Work

Your purpose in creating a legacy is not to convince everyone to think like you. It's not about maintaining control or using your knowledge to force others either subtly or overtly. Your legacy is about sharing, showing love, and freely giving of yourself. If others give freely in response, great. If not, they should not be pushed or coerced.

This may seem obvious, but parents do it all the time. They try to control their children's choices by withholding or giving money, applying guilt, and dictating how their kids dress, what career they select, and what religion they adopt. This is especially harmful as the children grow older and become adults. I've seen many fifty-year-olds who are still controlled by their parents either through guilt or money—and most express feelings of ineptness or resentment.

In *Family Wealth*, James E. Hughes writes about John D. Rockefeller's acceptance of his son's choice not to follow in his footsteps and become a businessman. "[T]his decision," he writes, "on the part of John Davison Rockefeller, Sr. to free his son to follow his individual pursuit of happiness is one of the most long-term wealth-preserving decisions in history."

Keep on your Meaning Legacy path. It can be disheartening when your children aren't enthusiastic about the family business or scoff at your stories of triumph, but don't be discouraged. There will be a time—maybe tomorrow, maybe fifty years from now—when your words and actions strike a chord. And the fact that you have taken the time to document them and preserve your legacy will become a priceless gift. Just think about it in your own life: Maybe you resisted your own father telling you what to do as a teenager, but now that you're older, you wish you had some of his advice written down somewhere.

A Prophet without Honor

"Jesus said to them, 'A prophet is not without honor, except in his own country, and among his own relatives, and in his own house.'"[8]

It used to drive my father crazy whenever my grandmother would complain to him, and he would come up with a solution that she'd ignore. Then, a few weeks later, she'd call him and say, "I've fixed that problem with the sprinklers. The neighbor said to buy metal sprinkler heads instead of the plastic ones."

"That's what I told you a month ago!" my dad would say.

"Oh, well, I don't remember that."

He'd bristle as he installed the new sprinkler heads for her.

And so it goes with those closest to you. One of the hardest things is establishing yourself as an expert to your own family. You may run multiple businesses, be a leader in your industry, and be a trusted confidant to your colleagues, but when you give advice to your spouse, he or she shrugs, says, "That's stupid. I'll call my friend. I think she'll know what to do." You may think this legacy thing is the best idea you've ever heard, and so you go to your family to discuss it. They roll their eyes, drag their feet, and don't see the point. No one takes it seriously.

There are two ways around this: The first is simply to be persistent and hope your family comes around once they see how interesting and powerful the idea is. It helps if you can convert one or two people to act as a cheerleader for your cause.

The second way is to bring in someone who specifically focuses on legacy planning. An expert becomes the spokesperson and ignites family members' interest. An expert-led family retreat or meeting gives you the benefit of being a participant and focusing on bonding with your family rather

---

8 Mark 6:4, *World English Bible* translation.

than trying to be the referee. Once the system is in place, then you can take it from there and create regular family events, with only the occasional tune-up from someone outside.

Feelings of Insignificance

If you feel like you don't have much wisdom to impart, it could be that you're not asking the right questions. I've interviewed all kinds of people who are the top in their fields and have made a tremendous impact. When I ask them about the legacy they'd like to leave behind, one of the most common responses I get is, "My life isn't that interesting." But then I dig deeper and am astounded by what I learn. A single insight from the unique perspective of someone who's experienced something beyond my peripheral gaze can elevate my thinking within an instant. One CEO told me that he couldn't think of any advice to give—and then five minutes later, he told me about a profound experience involving his brother delivering mail that I will forever remember when I think about how to manage my time. It's already altered the way I work.

I've also spoken with grandmothers who spent most of their adult lives at home, raising children, baking, and gardening. And their stories are just as important to their families as those from someone with a prestigious title or who has enjoyed fame or accolades. In fact, sometimes their stories are even more important because of how much they've interacted with their family and how loved they are.

Tell your story. Everyone has valuable stories and when you share your stories—in the right way—it changes the lives of your loved ones.

Vulnerability Is Tough

It's taken me a while to learn how powerful vulnerability can be. Although I still don't share every single detail of my life, I've gotten much better at opening up about my mistakes, as well as my hopes, dreams, and weird personality quirks. What it's led to is significantly closer relationships. When you open up to others, they feel safe to open up to you.

The way our loved ones respond to us often dictates what we feel comfortable sharing. If we feel judged or reprimanded—or know our stories will be used against us at some future date—we clam up. Sometimes this is a response to current company, and sometimes it's a programmed response from past relationships. Either way, I suggest practicing vulnerability with those you trust. And if you can't trust your loved ones, start working on ways to develop that trust. In Chapter 5, we cover how to create family rules and communication guidelines, which can be the first step to establishing a safe space to build trust.

Lead by being open. Your family cannot form a close relationship with you if you do not open up to them. Your mistakes make you human, and your quirks make you lovable. Without vulnerability, communication becomes superficial.

If you're used to closing off major parts of yourself, ask yourself why. Perhaps you want to protect your children by not telling them about the difficult times in your lives. Although this may make sense when a child is young and unable to process certain emotions, as children age, revealing hardships and how you navigated through them can give them hope and a chance to connect more deeply with you.

Fear of Loss of Choice or Independence

I have a colleague who assists widows with structuring their finances after they've lost their husbands. He says one of the most common issues he sees is the widow fearing that her adult children or others will try to undermine her decisions. It is a vulnerable time for her, and she must plan things right to get through the grieving process and new changes without compromising her future. If she can restructure her financial assets, transfer knowledge, and remain close with her family—all while maintaining control of her life—that is the best scenario and easily done with the correct process.

I also see this fear a lot with businesspeople. A man may have spent decades building up his company but refuses to share the details about it with his children. It's his "baby," and only he can run it. The problem is, of course, when the man ages or dies, his family is left to figure out something they don't understand—and his legacy dies with him.

Aging is scary, but we are all mortal. There is a natural order to things; with age comes the responsibility to mentor those who will come next. This is risky. You may be surpassed in some ways. You may feel like decisions are out of your control. So determine up front what areas you'd like to maintain control over—such as certain aspects of your business—and which areas you're fine with passing along—such as allowing your adult children to begin managing your nonprofit foundation or a certain project. Whether you maintain control or not, however, you need to plan for your obsolescence and think through how your family and employees will operate without you. They need the skills and training to be able to take over.

This is good for everyone. Your heirs will understand how to pick up where you left off, and you will transition into a role of a wise elder. Plus, there's the added benefit of more vacation time for you.

Mentorship has its own rhythm of give-and-take between mentor and mentee. Your mentee will teach you, too; you may be surprised by what you learn as you pass on your knowledge. Your children or younger employees are in their prime in a different era, with different experiences and worldviews. How they adapt and learn may be exactly what the company or your family needs to evolve.

Negative Outcomes for Heirs

Are you concerned that involving your family in active legacy planning will cause them harm? This concept comes up all the time in financial advising circles. "Don't let the kids know the family is rich" is a common strategy. Private wealth holders spend a lot of time worrying about how their success could hurt their children, or they try to protect them from hardships (and inadvertently end up protecting them from joy and how to cope with life as well).

James Grubman wrote an intriguing book about how families adapt to wealth across generations called *Strangers in Paradise*. He compares the "Land of Wealth" to a foreign country. Much like an immigrant needs to learn about the culture of their new home and adapt, families new to wealth are the same. They come from a middle-class background with its associated values (e.g., work ethic, independence, self-sufficiency, perseverance, managing your own assets) and must adapt to the new world of wealth (e.g., working with advisors, shared family decision-making, understanding partnerships, wealth literacy, philanthropy, and relationship skills).

Not just for the super wealthy, this concept applies to almost everyone in first-world nations. Adapting to a "new" culture is the burden of the next generation—especially in our rapidly changing world. Unless they are unusually hip, older people have no idea what apps teenagers are using. They don't understand how the workplace has changed or its pressures. The younger generation may feel overwhelmed at the prospect of having a family they can't support or school debt they can't pay back. Life is different for them than it was for their parents due to political, economic, and cultural changes.

In establishing your values, family identity, and communication, all generations must work together to create a well-adapted family. Just as children of an immigrant typically adapt more quickly to the new environment, new language, school, and social relationships than their parent does, the younger generations can add significant value from their unique perspective to adapt in a time of changing economics, technological advancements, new career models, and shifting societal family roles.

Desire for Privacy or Distrust of Others

If you've got substantial resources and financial assets, it's normal to want to protect them. Even if you don't consider yourself wealthy, your closely held values and stories ought to be respected. Those involved in family meetings and developing your legacy need to know your privacy protocol and have the emotional maturity to stick to it.

Guidelines will help everyone be clear and protect one

another. For example, if your family meets once a quarter to discuss your real estate holdings and other joint investments, those in the meeting need to know what can and cannot be discussed outside the family. A process of education is important to establish standards and introduce new members (such as spouses or partners) into the family.

People commonly share their private lives on social media. Determine what's not okay to share, and be sure those you trust with this information are aware of the boundaries.

Balancing Independence with Unity

In the US, independence is highly valued. When children are small, they depend upon their parents for financial and emotional support, but as they grow, they learn to become more independent until, one day, they leave the nest and start a life of their own.

It's crucial to properly balance having a close, supportive family with fostering independence. A family legacy should focus on the good parts of having a strong family foundation—a support system, love, principles, and connection—while pushing an individual pursuit of personal self-actualization.

The best legacies are organic and elastic. Your personal path and your own family (spouse and kids) should take precedence over complying with past family traditions. There is a natural separation that occurs when you find your own way. A great legacy isn't about creating a structure for your family to stay exactly as it is; it is a resource to help those you love grow and evolve on their own to create their individual legacies.

When to Start

"The best time to plant a tree was twenty years ago. The second-best time is now."
—Chinese proverb

Whether you have many years in front of you or are at the sunset of your life, your legacy is important. You are never too young or old. The approach you take, however, depends on where you are on your time line.

If you have young children, for example, your approach could focus on experiences to help them learn solid values and act with kindness, responsibility, and gratitude. If you have grandchildren, you could emphasize the wisdom you can share rather than creating daily habits and systems.

The sad, unpredictable reality is that you never know how long you will live or in what mental state you'll be. You could die tomorrow or go on for another three decades. You could be sharp as a tack until you're a centenarian or feel yourself slipping into Alzheimer's at seventy-five. Life is fleeting. Seize the moment.

Times to Start a Meaning Legacy

You can start your legacy at any point, but some of the most common times people decide to create a more formal legacy are:

Marriage or long-term partnership: It makes sense for you to work out your joint legacy as a couple so you can get on the same page before you begin having children or making big plans for the future.

Birth: When a new child comes into the world, this is often a time of reflection and planning. When you become a parent, grandparent, or aunt or uncle, a new sense of responsibility is placed upon you to help that little one feel loved and grow up to be independent, responsible, passionate, kind, and giving.

Divorce or separation: This is a great time to start a new legacy vision. If you have children, consider reaffirming your love for them and establishing new rules around how you will parent.

Remarriage and blending of families: Blending a family can be challenging. Getting everyone to contribute to a family legacy vision will make things much less hectic as well as dramatically improve communication, loyalty, and teamwork.

Educating children: Is it time for your children to go to school, or are they transitioning between grades? Don't rely on the school system to teach your kids about life. (Even if it's a swanky private school.) Establish values, morals, and a code of conduct for your children to follow as they grow and learn.

Dealing with health problems: This could be in old age or when you are younger. Either way, a health scare often causes us to think about just how fragile life is.

Caring for an elderly parent: Many people want to document their parents' lives as they age. This is also a great time to look at your own legacy and decide what you want to leave behind when you reach your parents' age.

Transition of a business: Successfully transferring a business—especially a family business—takes careful planning and documentation as you train your successors. It's also a great time to look within and consider what you want to do with your life now that your business is not your primary focus.

College graduation or starting a new career: Start your

career off right with an overall vision and a set of principles to guide you as you move toward your goals.

A new job or loss of a job, or sudden financial reversal: This can be the perfect time to plan for your legacy as you address this period of uncertainty.

To boost a business, project, or philanthropic initiative: A well-known public legacy can help you create more deal flow, attract funding, and build your influence.

Retirement: If planned right, retirement can be a period of growth, learning, and contribution.

Death: The death of a loved one causes us to value life that much more. Their memory—especially if documented right—can be a source of inspiration for living life to the fullest and planning what we are going to pass on when we are no longer here.

To Start Now: Take the Legacy Planning Assessment

*Visit **www.meaninglegacytools.com** to take the free legacy planning assessment to determine how you can structure your legacy plan for your specific circumstances.*

3

Stages of Legacy Maturity
Progressing to Wisdom

"Science is organized knowledge. Wisdom is organized life."
—Immanuel Kant, German philosopher

When I asked fundraiser Jeremy Gregg[9] about the mindset of his donors, he said, "It's all about Maslow's hierarchy of needs. Many of the nonprofits I raise money for help people on the lower rungs—people who need food, shelter, and clean water. But our donors, they're different. They are much higher up on the hierarchy. They are searching for a sense of purpose." He paused. "Finding a sense of purpose is definitely a first-world problem, but I don't know what's worse. In some ways, not having a purpose leaves you much more miserable than being without food."

A single mother working two minimum-wage jobs with only $163 in her savings account doesn't have the luxury of sitting around and pondering the meaning of life. She is fo-

---

9 www.jeremygregg.com

cused on paying her bills, taking care of her children, and trying to survive another day. Affluence gives us options, buying
us freedom to pursue our desires.

So the question then becomes: Once your basic survival
needs are taken care of, how do you spend the rest of your
time?

- Do you spend it acquiring more stuff (e.g., cars, homes,
  a boat)?

- Do you spend it on experiences (e.g., vacations, roman-
  tic dinners, surfing, playing tag football with the kids)?

- Do you spend it on hobbies (e.g., collecting stamps,
  learning guitar, painting)?

- Do you spend it on spiritual pursuits (e.g., meditation,
  church activities, religious study)?

- Do you spend it on learning (e.g., reading, getting another degree, going to seminars)?

- Do you spend it on service (e.g., feeding the homeless,
  visiting neighbors, philanthropic activities)?

- Do you spend it on escapism (e.g., television, video
  games, mind-altering substances)?

I believe all the above activities have their place, but the
ultimate purpose of life is inner development, and not for
the sole purpose of monetary success, fame, or an enhanced
reputation. I'm talking about authentic character building—
development for the sake of advancing one's state of being
and increasing love. It is from this paradigm that my team
approaches legacy development. To me, the greatest legacy is
how one has lived his or her life. If you have crafted yourself
into someone who is kind, intelligent, passionate, productive,

and courageous, that is the mark of a truly exemplary legacy.

Some things cannot be taught; they must be experienced. In your journey through legacy development, it's typical to go through the stages outlined in the coming pages. Where you are on the continuum is not necessarily a function of age; it's a matter of understanding and inner progression. It's not uncommon to bounce between stages or be more advanced in one area (like in your career) and less advanced in another (like being a parent).

Having a vision of what you would like your legacy to be will help you progress through the stages.

Stage 1: Innocence

At this stage, we focus on the beliefs, thoughts, values, attitudes, and assumptions taught to us by our parents and others in childhood. Many of these beliefs are subconscious and are thought to be "the way things are." You get stuck in the mindset that "money doesn't grow on trees" because your father always told you that. Or you believe your best path forward is to become a nurse because all the women in your family are nurses. You follow a path laid out by your family because you don't know any better and breaking out of the cultural or family norm is scary. You live your life for others, and your main objective is to be accepted by the community.

Stage 2: Inner Conflict

Your beliefs in the "innocence" stage are questioned, and this creates discord within you, producing difficult emotions. It leads to conflict, guilt, shame, and distance from the community or your family's wishes. You desire to follow your heart, break away, and make your own path, but it's scary—there's no model for you to follow, and questioning "the way things are" could cause you to make mistakes, be ostracized, or feel foolish.

Stage 3: Navigating

Bracken Darrell, Harvard graduate and CEO of Logitech, told me, "A lot of people don't know how to identify their passions, but what I tell my kids is that finding your passion is like going on a road trip. You will be so much more successful if you select a destination—even if you don't ultimately end up there. If you don't have a destination, you just go around in circles."

That's what this stage is all about. You decide to set your own path and start making your journey toward specific goals. Along the way, you identify your resources, skills, virtues, moral conduct, and rules to live by.

Stage 4: Resilience

Life will throw curve balls. You'll learn that sometimes your goals don't work out; sometimes, life is a mess due to illness, financial disaster, betrayal, addiction, or a host of other problems. Eventually, after trying to control what can't be controlled, you learn that life is about creating happiness amid anxiety, stress, and suffering.

Stage 5: Engagement

At this stage, you've figured out some stuff. You know what

makes you happy and you have the freedom to pursue your passions. You understand the ebb and flow of life and have learned how to cultivate energy, enthusiasm, and faith. You experience success through accomplishing goals, earning money, and pushing through adversity.

Stage 6: Vision

This is when your life purpose extends beyond yourself to your community or family. You begin to see your connection with and influence on others, and you desire to make their lives better, along with your own. Your success, money, and passions become a conduit through which you affect the world. This is when your legacy becomes something that truly matters to you—not as a way to get ahead or improve yourself, but as a way to help others.

Stage 7: Wisdom

The final stage is a place of wisdom and generosity. You have made it through all the stages and have the luxury of being able to look back on your life with perspective.

Your Outlook

Let's look at how each stage affects your outlook. I recommend keeping a legacy journal while answering the following questions.

Don't be concerned if you're stuck in a certain stage. Sometimes you need to stay in a stage for quite some time;

if you're investing all your time in starting your business and stressed about paying your bills, for example, you're not at a point to focus on being a wise mentor. You've got to ensure your own stability first. This isn't about pushing yourself toward the final goal; it's about systematically refining your legacy and sculpting a better character as you go along. Simply understanding the stages and asking the right questions will help you focus on ways to move from one stage to the next.

Stage 1: Innocence

In innocence, you are making decisions on autopilot based on your conditioning. To progress beyond this mindset, you must first identify which beliefs came from your parents, teachers, religious leaders, or other influential people and if they're something you buy into now. People stuck in this stage often blindly go along with whatever their family has planned for them, or they make decisions based on subconscious conditioning.

Ask these questions to help yourself see a little more clearly your own influences:

- What are my parents' values?

- What kinds of beliefs did I learn as a child that I no longer have?

- What did I like about growing up (and would like to emulate)?

- What didn't I like about growing up?

- Who were my mentors and teachers growing up? What did they teach me? Does their philosophy still apply to my life?

Stage 2: Inner Conflict

This is when you want to break away from deep-seated beliefs but experience discord because of fear of breaking away or possibly not pleasing others with your actions.

Ask these questions to start identifying what feels authentic to you:

- When do I do things that go against my gut?
- When don't I speak up for myself?
- When do I let others make decisions for me?
- When do I compare myself to others?
- When do I judge others? (Your judgment of others is typically a reflection of criticism you feel about yourself.)

Stage 3: Navigating

Here, you break out on your own and pick a destination for yourself by outlining goals and principles that resonate with you.

Ask these questions of yourself:

- What actions make me feel good?
- What actions make me feel bad/guilty?
- What is my role in my family/with my friends/in the community?
- What is worth fighting for?
- What do I believe to be true?
- What am I passionate about?

- What am I most grateful for?

During this stage, select several heroes or people who exemplify the kind of person you want to be and model their good traits. Read books that feed your soul and contain timeless wisdom; they will keep you grounded and embed stories in your mind so you can cope with struggles when they inevitably come up.

Some of my favorite texts are:

- *Man's Search for Meaning* by Viktor E. Frankl
- *The Power of Myth* by Joseph Campbell
- *Letters from a Stoic* by Seneca
- *Meditations* by Marcus Aurelius
- *The Art of Being* by Erich Fromm
- *The Holy Bible*
- *Siddhartha* by Hermann Hesse
- *The Story of Art* by E. H. Gombrich
- *The Alchemist* by Paulo Coelho
- *The Brothers Karamazov* by Fyodor Dostoyevsky

This is just a small smattering. Go with what interests you—poetry, theater, anthropology, science, religion, history, literature, mythology, or art. As you delve into these texts, you will begin to see patterns among philosophies or beliefs that will resonate with you. Record your thoughts in your journal.

Stage 4: Resilience

At this stage, you will experience some disappointments, and your ability to grow from them will turn you into a stronger person. Making the commitment to never give up is 90 percent of the battle.

One of the founders of post-traumatic growth, Lawrence Calhoun, PhD, spent years studying survivors of severe injuries. He found that survivors of crisis typically grow in five specific ways. These growth points apply to not only overcoming injuries but also anything challenging, from divorce to bankruptcy to extreme loss.

The five benefits of overcoming a crisis are:

1. The emergence of new possibilities or opportunities

2. Increased emotional strength

3. Positive changes in relationships

4. Greater appreciation for life

5. Spiritual development

As you learn how to accept unexpected outcomes and see the beauty in them, your life becomes fuller and happier.

Ask these questions of yourself:

- What can I learn from this trauma/crisis/mistake?

- What kind of thinking led me to this disaster?

- In what ways can I choose happiness no matter my outer circumstances?

Stage 5: Engagement

The engagement stage is a great place to be. You've figured out how to be in "the zone," at least for a good part of the time. And you push forward with faith and tenacity toward what brings you joy.

Ask these questions of yourself:

- What gives me peace and joy?

- What is meaningful to me?

- Do I know the difference between working for a wage and my calling?

- How can I more fully experience this current moment?

- In what ways can I take care of myself (e.g., meditation, a walk on the beach)?

This is what the mindfulness movement is all about. Personally, I pay attention to what energizes me—which is mostly writing, teaching, studying, and creating. Each person has his or her own loves. Following that bliss takes you to new levels of joy.

Stage 6: Vision

At this stage, it's not just about what makes you happy. You also concern yourself with giving to those around you and creating a vision that will impact your family and community.

Ask these questions of yourself:

- How can I serve?

- How can I best leverage my talents, skills, and resources to help others?

- How can I inspire?

- How do I want to be remembered?

- What do I appreciate about people in my life?

People at this stage get that they are here for a reason, which is to help others in a way that aligns with their own personal journey.

Stage 7: Wisdom

You have arrived. You have something to contribute—wisdom, skills, and perspective you've gained along the way. Your example and vision has resulted in a legacy that your family and the community respects. This is the stage at which Andrew Carnegie gave away his fortune. It's also the stage where many people want to become involved in mentoring, giving to a cause, or teaching their grandchildren.

Ask these questions of yourself:

- How do I want my name to live on?

- What are ways I can help future generations grow and evolve by passing on my wisdom and resources?

- When I think back to the earlier stages of my life, which methods helped me grow and evolve?

- How can I spread that knowledge to others?

In the next chapter, we'll review how to define your beliefs and design a vision for your personal legacy progression.

PART 2

COMPONENTS OF A
MEANING LEGACY

4

Personal Beliefs, Values, and Vision

Happiness and Ethics

"It is not living that matters, but living rightly."

—Socrates, classical Greek philosopher

In 2011, University of Missouri economist Harvey James[10] analyzed survey results from hundreds of thousands of people in the United States, Canada, Mexico, and Brazil. What he found is that people who reported having a more ethical view (i.e., they answered on the survey that they believed cheating on your taxes or accepting a bribe was wrong) also reported having a higher satisfaction with life than those who were not bothered by less ethical acts.

Your character plays a large role in how you perceive the world and how it perceives you. Takers are looked down upon

---

10 Harvey S. James, Jr., "Is the Just Man a Happy Man? An Empirical Study of the Relationship Between Ethics and Subjective Well-Being," *Kyklos* 64, no. 2 (2011): 193–212.

in a society that must function with the cooperation of others. Those who build lasting and loving friendships, marriages, and business ties are dependable, trustworthy, compassionate, just, and emotionally intelligent.

Most people, however, need to learn how to achieve higher levels of moral behavior. In one study[11] regarding this phenomenon, students were divided into groups based on age, and the group that made the most ethical decisions was the oldest (age 40-plus), followed in order by the next oldest age groups. The least ethical decisions were made by the youngest students (age 21 years or younger).

As we age, we learn how our decisions can potentially hurt others, how to become more empathetic, and what actions make us feel good or bad. Without a process or a set of principles to guide us along this journey, life can get confusing—and sometimes painful. Think of all the amazing people with so much potential who took a wrong turn that led to a less-than-desirable legacy. They cheated on a spouse and destroyed their families. They got caught up in drugs or alcohol or another addiction. They operated in the gray zone of legality and lost their freedom or reputation. Or they simply lived a life of quiet desperation, lacking joy and meaning. To reach a destination of happiness, contentment, fulfillment, and passion, we must know what we want and constantly correct our path to get there.

A lot of people can definitively say what they think they want, especially if they're high achievers: a big home, a Porsche, a thriving career, a happy family, travel, and so on. But how often do we think about what we want from a spiri-

---

11 Durwood Ruegger, Ernest W. King, "A Study of the Effect of Age and Gender upon Student Business Ethics," *Journal of Business Ethics* 11, no. 3 (March 1992): 179–186.

tual or values-based viewpoint? And how often is that vision articulated well enough to measure one's ethical progression? In this chapter, we will discuss how to define your beliefs and construct a meaningful vision for your personal legacy.

Your Personal Legacy Statement

Your Personal Legacy Statement is your declaration of how you'd like to live your life and impact others from an ethical standpoint. It's different from goals, which are about achievements. The objective of a Personal Legacy Statement is to clearly state your principles, how you intend to treat others, how you plan to care for your spiritual needs, and how you will share your legacy.

Seneca[12] wrote, "Cherish some man of high character, and keep him ever before your eyes, living as if he were watching you, and ordering all your actions as if he beheld them. . . . For we must indeed have someone according to whom we may regulate our characters; you can never straighten that which is crooked unless you use a ruler."

Whether you have an actual person you hold yourself accountable to or base your principles on traits you respect in a variety of individuals, the key to developing an effective Personal Legacy Statement is identifying the ideal character you wish to cultivate and progressing toward that end.

---

12 Lucius Annaeus Seneca, *Letters from a Stoic*, Letter 11.

The Legacy Paradox

Creating a great legacy presents an interesting paradox: The whole point of one is to positively affect others, yet if you let others dictate how you live, your legacy will feel hollow.

The single most important thing I can tell you about developing your Personal Legacy Statement is that you need to spend time alone evaluating what you want. Don't compare yourself to your friends on Facebook. Don't think about the new car your neighbors just bought or the Ivy League college that just accepted their son. Don't worry about how your mother will respond. Don't think about how your husband will laugh.

Think about what matters to you—and only you. No one lives in a vacuum, of course; you have obligations, decisions you've made that lead to responsibilities, people you interact with. But you're not here to please everyone else. You are here to find your calling and live in a way that expands your soul.

Following Your Wiser Self

Your Wiser Self is that inner voice of wisdom. It's expansive, imaginative, self-aware, and confident. It focuses on the long-term results of your actions and directs you to make choices to bring you more love, joy, and fulfillment. It's not motivated by fear or ego; its purpose is to turn you into an exemplary man or woman—one you respect, who has a strong character, and who does the right thing. Great legacies are a result of following the direction of your Wiser Self.

If you are experiencing pain, confusion, or purposelessness, ask your Wiser Self why. The answer could be immediate or it could take time through journaling, introspection, counseling, study, or meditation. When you make time to check in with your Wiser Self, your perspective changes, resulting in a more authentic legacy.

Developing Your Personal Legacy Statement

A Personal Legacy Statement is yours. You will consult with your Wiser Self and touch base with your inner world, a world you may have not shared with anyone. Maybe you have a spouse or someone you trust enough to share it with, but this is about keeping yourself on track. We'll discuss how to make parts of it public and how to lead your family and community improvement efforts a bit later. But your Personal Legacy Statement is about putting your values, principles, and beliefs—not to mention your heart and soul—on paper.

When I first wrote my Personal Legacy Statement, I specifically focused on adding extra phrases that helped me overcome personal weaknesses or struggles. This served as a reminder to me to pay extra attention to those things so I didn't fall into old, destructive habits.

Letting others read these kinds of phrases is like standing naked before them. If you don't feel free to openly express your deepest desires and admit your struggles without fearing judgement, you'll edit yourself. And the last thing you want is a watered-down, politically correct, vanilla Legacy Statement. You may have a polished version the world sees, but give yourself the freedom to write something that goes deep.

Because your life is always in a state of flux, your Personal Legacy Statement will evolve with you. As you regularly refer back to it, some areas will begin feeling inauthentic or they may need more clarification. Rewrite it as often as you see fit. And don't get stuck on making your statement perfect to begin with. Just get something down in writing and start using it. You will perfect it as you go along.

The following three-step process is what my company uses to develop a Legacy Statement. Write down your thoughts in a journal or type them out. These ideas will lead to your final statement.

Step 1: Identify Your Roles

The first step in creating your Legacy Statement is to identify your different life roles and how you'd like to represent yourself in each one. Write down how you envision yourself fulfilling each of the following roles:

> Role 1: Family Role—How do you wish to connect with and love those in your family? Think about your role as a grandparent, a parent, a spouse, a son or daughter, a grandchild, or an aunt or uncle.

> Role 2: Social Role—How do you want to interact with friends and acquaintances? How do you wish to have fun with them and show them you care?

> Role 3: Career Role—How do you want to impact those you work with? How do you find passion and enjoyment in your career? Do you have a larger vision about how you want to serve others through your work?

> Role 4: Community Role—How will you contribute to your neighbors and local community? Do you have a pas-

sion for helping a certain group of people or furthering a cause?

Role 5: Spiritual Role—How will you nourish your spirit or need for creativity, connection, rest, and balance? How will you grow yourself? How will you care for your body and well-being?

Step 2: Define Your Principles

Your legacy should consider the ends and the means. If your burning desire is to help others, you could steal bread from grocery stores and give it to the poor. Helping the poor would be a noble cause. Stealing bread, on the other hand, may not be the most principled way to get to that end.

You need a value system to go along with your end vision. If you want to help others ethically, your value system must specify that you will not harm anyone else in the process.

Spend some time thinking about what values and morals will help you fulfill your various roles. Consider these questions as you're writing down the values that matter to you:

- What principles are important to follow to fulfill the roles you've outlined for yourself?

- Which character attributes are most important to you?

- Are there personal weaknesses or struggles that will make it hard for you to fulfill your legacy if you don't address them?

Step 3: Specify How You Wish to Share Your Legacy

You know when someone says something profound and it gives you chills, but then a few hours later, you can't even remember what they said? When I interviewed futurist Daniel Burrus, he said one of the most important things you can do to preserve meaningful moments is to stop and document something significant when it happens. These moments must be documented or else they are lost. Memories fade quickly; what gets remembered is what is recorded and shared. This third step is about stopping and realizing what you've created with your life.

Consider these questions when thinking about how you wish to share your legacy:

- How will you record and document meaningful experiences?

- How will you let others know how much they mean to you? (For example, will you write them a letter to express your appreciation?)

- How will you mentor others or pass on your wisdom or skills?

Reviewing Your Progress

There are a variety of ways to measure your progress, but one of the simplest and most effective ways is to refer back to your Legacy Statement regularly and compare it to your behavior.

After only a short time of regularly consulting my Legacy Statement, I could feel my behavior changing. It was like a gentle reprogramming of my thoughts. When tempted to take an action that was not in alignment with my outlined principles, I'd change course or feel really guilty if I chose something that didn't represent who I wanted to be.

I want my life to be positively focused, for example, and when I obsess over negative thoughts or begin gossiping about someone, a phrase from my Legacy Statement comes to mind:

I keep my life simple, free from clutter, disorder, and things that steal my energy for negative purposes (e.g., addictions, gossip, worry, trivial concerns).

This simple phrase, in many instances, has the power to stop me in my tracks and redirect my behavior to align with the kind of person I want to be. That's the power a Legacy Statement can have. It serves as the ruler Seneca spoke of.

In Chapter 10, we'll discuss more concrete steps you can take to progress toward your ideal legacy.

Example of Private Personal Legacy Statement

The following is an example of a legacy statement written for private use. It's quite long; often, legacy statements start off as more verbose simply because you're getting your thoughts down on paper and evaluating what is and isn't important to you. As you refine your ideas, it may make sense to edit it down to something shorter that represents your vision more concisely.

My Principles

Integrity: In all I do, I endeavor to act in the best interest of all parties involved and exercise integrity with my personal and business dealings.

Being a Giver: I give of myself first in any new relationship and operate under the assumption that the other person is a giver until experience proves otherwise. I forgive others for their mistakes and try to understand things from their point of view.

Positive Thinking/Speaking: I focus on the positive attributes of others. When I speak to or about another person, I never say something for the sole purpose of hurting them or blemishing their reputation.

Responsibility: I do not blame outside circumstances or others for my mistakes or problems. When something bad happens, I see the role I played and admit to my part. I also treat others' possessions and public spaces as if they were my own and exercise the same kind of care. I don't expect others to clean up after me or take care of my needs.

Humility: Everyone has their own brand of intelligence. Everyone fights a battle. I am not better than others. There is always something to learn from those around me. Sometimes I'm on top, sometimes I'm at rock bottom, sometimes I act smart, sometimes I act like an idiot—just like everyone else does.

Order: I keep my life simple, free from clutter, disorder, and things that steal my energy for negative purposes (e.g., addictions, gossip, worry, trivial concerns).

Curiosity: I am open to all kinds of outcomes. When things don't go my way, I act as a third-party observer and try to see my situation from a state of curiosity rather than disappointment.

Action in Spite of Discomfort: When I know something is right, I immediately take action, even if it's hard or causes short-term discomfort.

Self-Compassion: When I make mistakes, I forgive myself and have compassion for my shortcomings. I create an environment for myself that is safe, healthy, and caring. When I need help, I ask for it.

Fun/Adventure: Life should be passionate and engaging. I see the wondrous every day. The ordinary becomes extraordinary to me because of how I love, who I interact with, and the joy of my pursuits.

Nourishing My Soul

Throughout the day, I take breaks to recharge myself. This includes running, working out, spending time in nature, meditation, baths, painting, writing for fun, or reading. I spend several hours a week thinking about ways to improve my character and learning about new concepts and ideas.

Family Role

My purpose in my family is to support my family members in their dreams, have fun with them, create lasting memories, be open and truthful, and be a good example.

Social Role

I focus on finding and cultivating deep friendships with people who have similar values and whom I admire and trust.

Career Role

I am responsible and pay my bills but focus on work that energizes me. My vision and calling is more important to me than simply earning a high wage. When working with clients, I endeavor to do what is best for them and, at the very least, do no harm.

Community Role

Every year, I review what I'm doing to help others to be sure I'm on track. I make an effort to meet new people from different backgrounds and learn from everyone I come into contact with.

My Health

I eat an unprocessed diet focused on vegetables, healthy fats, proteins, moderate fruit, and limited carbohydrates.

Every day, I move my body and expend enough energy to feel healthy, balanced, and in good shape.

Sharing My Legacy

I make an effort to document important life moments as they happen and store this documentation in a safe place. I write letters to those who inspire me either as it happens or once a year when I review the happenings of my life. I make a consistent effort to tell others how grateful I am to have them in my life, and I'm specific about what I appreciate about them.

More Examples of Personal Legacy Statements

The following are Personal Legacy Statements and mission statements from some recognizable and not-so-recognizable people. Most of these are polished and meant for public consumption. Once you've created your long, private Legacy Statement, you may want to create something shorter, in alignment with these examples. A shorter, public statement allows you to openly share your vision with friends, family and business associates.

> *To be honest, to be kind—to earn a little and to spend a little less, to make upon the whole a family happier for his presence, to renounce when that shall be necessary and not be embittered, to keep a few friends, but these without capitulation—above all, on the same grim condition, to keep friends with himself—here is a task for all that a man has of fortitude and delicacy.*

—Poet and writer Robert Louis Stevenson[13]

I will approach my life in a thoughtful and intelligent manner. I will treat people with compassion, kindness, and fairness. I will approach each day with energy, creativity, and humor. I will not forget to relax. I will keep the dance of delight in my life. I will not work too hard, and I will give time to literature and life.

My Family Role: I will conduct myself in family life in a manner that enriches our home by my presence. My family will be happy when I'm home. I will be a leader to my extended family.

My Work: I will influence people with example, in walking my talk, in principle-centered living.

My Role as a Citizen of the World: I hold the following principles: By the Grace of God; Forgiveness; Empowering Others; Growing a Garden of Empowerment; Diversity of Race and Culture Is a Gift; I will sustain life in physical, mental, emotional, and spiritual areas. To

---

13   Excerpt from his 1892 travel memoir, *Across the Plains.*

forgive myself more, and get on with doing good work.

—A. Roger Merrill[14]

To find happiness, fulfillment, and value in living, I will seek out and experience all of the pleasures and joys that life has to offer. My core values are not limitations restraining me on this hedonistic quest for fun. Rather, they provide a framework for identifying, pursuing, and achieving those pleasures that last the longest and are the most satisfying. The greatest joy of all is being worthy of the respect and admiration of family, friends, and business associates.

—Ronnie Max Oldham[15]

To serve God with all my heart, soul and mind (neither to burn out, nor rust our but to wear out for the Lord). It is my goal to 'die young at 80.' To accomplish this, I will keep actively involved with my family (children/ grandchildren) and with the youth of the Christian church. In addition, I will commit myself to continuing my education to remain stimulated and mentally active. It is my desire to be an excellent role model for my wife, family, business, clients and friends. This can only be accomplished with God's help, and it is my goal to daily read and study the scriptures to help me to this end. I pledge myself to be faithful to my wife, to love her unconditionally and to care for her forever. I value our differences and view them as strengths. I seek to build a complementary relationship with Chris. I value her life's experiences and seek to learn and grow from

---

14 Stephen R. Covey, *How to Develop Your Personal Mission Statement.*
15 Ronnie Max Oldham sells data integration solutions in Austin, Texas. His personal website (ronnieoldham.com) lists more information about his hobbies, travel, and interests.

her. It is my desire to be a Christ-like role model for my children. It is my desire to be more than a financial provider. It is my goal to be physically present at as many special events (games, concerts) in their lives as is possible. I hope to teach them to work and develop their unique talents, but to not take themselves too seriously. My motto which I hope to convey is 'don't sweat the small stuff, it's all small stuff.' I want to be fun-loving, forgiving, and love them unconditionally.

—Monroe M. Diefendorf, Jr., CEO of 3 Dimensional Wealth Advisory

---

In order for me to agree to a performance, it must:

1) Educate others

2) Entertain others

3) Make enough money I am not in want

4) Be something my grandmother would find respectable

5) Build healthy relationships

—Paul W. Draper[16]

I will follow my intuition and take immediate, bold action because that is the most loving way. I will only commit to things I can fulfill. I will speak with integrity and reveal my feelings openly and quickly, even if it is uncomfortable at times (and may not please everyone). I will only speak about others in a way that would make me comfortable if they were standing in the room.

---

16 Paul W. Draper is an anthropologist, academic, and award-winning mentalist, magician, and filmmaker. He can be found at mentalmysteries.com.

I will only take actions that move me towards the light. In all my actions, I will be honest, transparent and only do things that I would be proud to reveal to my closest friends and family.

I will approach each day with creativity, love, gratitude, curiosity and humor. I will not forget to take breaks and relax. My life will be focused on developing my soul and helping others evolve theirs. I will thoroughly enjoy the journey no matter what happens!

I will forgive quickly, apologize quickly when I have hurt someone and have great compassion for myself when I make mistakes. When I do make mistakes, I will look inward and use them to help me grow and learn.

Family Role: I will conduct myself in a way that makes my future children (and husband) proud. I will be loving, giving and supportive to my family. My presence will always uplift, but I will have the backbone to speak the truth in a kind but direct way even if it is sometimes uncomfortable.

Work: My focus will be on God's will and having fun! I will influence people with my example and have great integrity in all that I do. I will be guided by intuition and know that there is always a solution to any obstacle. When I commit to something, I will give it all of my attention and endeavor to deliver the highest quality possible. If I know that I cannot devote my time, heart and soul to an endeavor, I will pass on it. I will encourage and uplift others.

Citizen: I will strive to uplift those around me and take actions that benefit my community. I will use my skills and talents to serve. My focus will be on empowerment or bringing out the light in others, helping them recognize and expand their abilities and see their intrinsic value.

Health: I will move every day. I will eat foods that nourish my body, mind and soul. I will refrain from alcohol, drugs and other harmful substances. I will not be too uptight and will enjoy life!

—Anonymous Client

To love God and love others.

—Joel Manby, CEO of Herschend Family Entertainment[17]

To be a teacher. And to be known for inspiring my students to be more than they thought they could be.

—Oprah Winfrey[18]

To have fun in [my] journey through life and learn from [my] mistakes.

—Sir Richard Branson, founder of the Virgin Group[19]

To use my gifts of intelligence, charisma, and serial optimism to cultivate the self-worth and net worth of women around the world.

—Amanda Steiberg, founder of DailyWorth[20]

---

17 Stephanie Vozza, "Personal Mission Statements of 5 Famous CEOs (And Why You Should Write One Too)," *Fast Company* (February 25, 2014).
18 Drew Hendricks, "Personal Mission Statement of 13 CEOs and Lessons You Need to Learn," *Forbes* (November 10, 2014).
19 "Sir Richard Branson: On a Mission to Mentor," *Motivated Magazine* (May 4, 2011).
20 Vozza, "Personal Mission Statements."

*To constantly evolve myself, have fun, and lift up oth-
ers through kindness, curiosity, and creativity.*

—Laura Roser[21]

---

21 This is my shorter public statement. I started with the longer version referenced
earlier in this chapter—which I still read regularly and periodically update.

5

Family Beliefs, Values, and Vision

Steve Jobs's Greatest Regret

"If you bungle raising your children, I don't think whatever else you do matters very much."

—Jacqueline Kennedy Onassis, wife of the 35th President of the United States

Walter Isaacson, Steve Jobs's biographer, asked the tech giant if he had any regrets. Jobs said, "I wanted my kids to know me. I wasn't always there for them, and I wanted them to know why and to understand what I did." Isaacson went on to ask him if he was glad that he'd had kids, and Jobs said, "It's 10,000 times better than anything I've ever done."

Most people go into parenthood with good intentions. They want their kids to succeed and be happy and healthy. But life often gets in the way of good intentions. You work late rather than attending your son's football game. You lose your temper when the kids are screaming like banshees. You refuse to speak to your husband after you find out he was flirting with a woman at the office. A business deal goes south and you let down your employees and family. Life is full of sticky situations. If you're not careful, feelings are hurt and never repaired, guilt sets in, and family dinnertime becomes an emotional warzone.

How do you keep your family on track? You need to build a joint belief system, a way to work through conflicts, and commitment to each other. This strong family foundation doesn't happen by accident. It must be built with purposeful devotion.

Now is a confusing time for many because the concept of family or community is changing dramatically. Recent studies[22] have shown that fewer people are attending church or identifying themselves with a specific religion. And, according to the US census, in 1960, 72 percent of people aged 18 or older were married. Today, that number has dropped to 50.2 percent.

Neighborhoods aren't what they used to be either. Recent data from the General Social Survey[23] found that only 20 percent of Americans spent time with their neighbors in the last thirty days. Four decades ago, a third of the population hung out with their neighbors twice a week.

They say it takes a village to raise a child, but where do you find your village? Certainly, your neighbors are too busy. And if you don't go to church, where does your village of people with common values, traditions, and beliefs exist?

I've spoken with many childless singles and couples, and I've found there is a rising concern about having the ability

---

22 Daniel Burke, "Millennials Leaving Church in Droves, Study Finds," *CNN* (May 14, 2015), http://www.cnn.com/2015/05/12/living/pew-religion-study/index.html.
23 Joe Cortright, "Less in Common," *City Reports* (September 6, 2015), http://cityobservatory.org/less-in-common/.

to raise children correctly. One man told me he was worried about having children because he didn't think he could give his kids the kind of upbringing his parents gave him.

"When I grew up," he said, "we lived in a close neighborhood. All the kids played together. I was surrounded by my cousins and extended family. I just don't see many options to replicate that experience."

It's not all bad. There are reasons people are moving away from tradition. Over time, as society changes, it makes sense to explore new models. But you don't want your children's thinking manipulated by random sources that don't align with your values. You need solid principles to help mold your family. If your kids don't get direction from you, they'll get it by accident—from friends, school, television, the internet, or whoever crosses their path.

It's not enough to tell your kids to follow the golden rule or be a good person. How are they going to handle sex? What about spiritual development? How are they going to deal with dishonesty or manipulation? How will they be motivated to follow their passions? How will they know when to follow the rules and when to break them? Someone needs to teach them this stuff.

Coventry Edwards-Pit wrote a book called *Raised Healthy, Wealthy & Wise* in which she and her team interviewed a series of children from exceptionally wealthy families. In these interviews, it was determined there were four main components that successfully launched children into adult life:

1. Demonstrate an ability to earn their own money.

2. Motivate themselves to achieve personal goals.

3. Create a solid sense of self not wrapped up in issues related to wealth.

4. Overcome setbacks and learn from failure.

You will undoubtedly have your own set of criteria. What do you believe are the most important attributes your children need when they leave the nest? How do you create a supportive environment to encourage these attributes? That leads us to defining your family identity.

Your Family Identity

Your family identity comprises the following components:

- Values
- Mantra
- Family mission
- Family rules
- Coat of arms or logo

Even though your family is not a company, you can think of this process as similar to creating a business brand and culture. When your family knows what it represents and there's a level of accountability involved, it functions to support that vision.

The Inner Circle

Before you begin determining what's important to your family, first define who is a part of your "inner circle." Is it immediate family only? What about an ex-spouse, a close friend, nieces and nephews, or a long-term partner? Who do you want to participate in family planning for things like family vacations, day-to-day activities, and financial decisions?

It helps if your inner-circle family members live in the same home or are otherwise close, but there are no rules. You can define your family however you like. One of the closest families I know comprises a single mother, her unmarried brother, her son, and her mother. Another family video conferences with each other from around the globe.

Growing up, my family on my father's side was close. We spent holidays and family vacations together. I knew my cousins and grandparents very well. Still, while I was living at home, my core family—my parents, brothers, and sister—were the "inner circle." This is because we wanted our own identity apart from what my grandparents had established; we wanted to create systems and processes for our home that were separate from what aunts or uncles did with their children.

It's best to begin creating your family identity as early as possible. Once your kids are grown, it's much harder to mold family dynamics. The following are the five best times to create a family identity:

1. When you are first married (or declare a long-term partnership).

2. When you are pregnant or have your first child.

3. When your children are young (ages one through twelve).

4. When your children are teenagers. (This is on the edge; some kids are receptive, while others are not. But, at the very least, you can provide a model for when they have their own families.)

5. When you have a big change in the family while your children are still young. (For example, divorce, a blending of families, or an introduction of a new stepparent or long-term partner.)

Do You Have Adult Children?

If you are older with adult children, this process can still work for you—especially if you have a close family. Many families want to cultivate loving relationships with cousins, aunts, and uncles. The main difference from starting when your children are young versus when they are older is your personal control. By the time your children are grown, they have their own ideas about how they'd like to live and parent. Your role is to support their choices.

Your influence in the day-to-day molding of the family will be limited because it becomes your children's role as parents to manage their own families. Even if your adult children do not have a spouse or children, your role should include promoting independence and healthy autonomy.

Another important thing: If you have substantial wealth or businesses to transfer to your heirs, the sooner you create a governance process, the better. Don't wait for a crisis or a total breakdown in communication, which tends to happen when family members are not on the same page. It can get extremely complicated with spouses, grandchildren, and other family members all voicing their opinions. It's best to communicate your vision accurately and definitively now.

Seed Questions

Let's jump into the family identification process. The best way to start is by simply discussing ideas. An open family narrative is just as important, if not more important, than the creation of your actual plan. This is not a dictatorship; everyone in the family needs to contribute. In my company's workshops, we emphasize the importance of creating a trusting environment in which family members can be respected and feel heard. To get buy-in, everyone must participate.

One exception here is small children. Give them as much responsibility as they can handle and, as they grow, give them more opportunities to participate. Maybe your three-year-old can pick out a song for your family meeting, but your eight-year-old contributes to the family discussion and gives feedback about what is and isn't working with the family.

If you have significant financial assets and are interested in a family governance process to manage these assets, it's best to bring in a financial firm to assist. Although the process[24] we

---

24 Creating a vision for the family business or significant financial assets is different than the process we are about to cover, which is to establish values and a mission within your family and involve all family members in its creation. When we're talking about asset distribution, the initial vision needs to come from the top—the people who built the business or who oversee the assets—because they are the most knowledgeable and need to feel comfortable handing over those assets to competent heirs. They can then work with younger generations or their heirs to take over. If you need help with family governance in relation to significant financial assets, I suggest finding a firm that

are about to cover can lay the foundation for family communication, it isn't meant for financial asset management.

The First Meeting

To start, gather everyone together around the dinner table or in the living room. Make sure to have a whiteboard or an oversized notepad with markers handy.

If you don't currently have children, these basic questions will help you begin:

- How do we each view the relationship?

- How do we deal with differences and conflict?

- Do we want children? If yes, what kind of parents do we want to be?

- How will we prepare our children to lead good lives?

- Do we want to work with our existing family traditions, or do we want to create new traditions?

If you have children, here are some basic questions to ask the family and brainstorm answers to:

- What is most important to us as a family?

- What are our unique talents, gifts, or abilities?

- Are there things we don't like about our family? If so, how should we change them?

- What principles do we want to follow as a family?

- What do we want our family to be known for?

---

specializes in it. Make sure its focus is family communication, not setting up structures to control heirs.

Answering these questions gets the family talking. Sometimes ideas flow, and as you discuss, a family belief system will begin to take shape. Other times, it can be uncomfortable. If your family isn't used to talking openly about their feelings, it can take time to tease out. Don't get frustrated— it's natural for there to be some discomfort simply because introspection of this kind may be a new activity. But it's well worth it. The families who have been through creating a family identity and all that goes with it often say that it is one of the most profound things they have ever done with their families. Spend time talking as long as it's fun and productive. If it gets tense or too long, table the discussion and pick it up at another time.

Family Values

Now that we've talked about what is and what is not important to the family, let's define some values. Have your family look at the words below (or come up with your own) and ask, "What words best describe our family or who we aspire to be?"

Resilient	Persevering	Purposeful
Courageous	Faithful	Persistent
Passionate	Authentic	Enthusiastic
Forgiving	Responsible	Authentic
Blissful	Just	Excited
Curious	Compassionate	Meaningful
Inventive	Loving	Motivated by

growth	Committed	Self-controlled
Joyful	Generous	Well-mannered
Creative	Loyal	Hopeful
Imaginative	Good-natured	Open-minded
Unique	Adventurous	Wise
Surprised	Insatiable	Knowledgeable
Independent	Adaptable	Eloquent
Community focused	Happy	Brave
	Optimistic	Kind
Limitless	Unforgettable	Down to earth
Diverse	Feisty	Leaders
Innovative	Fun-loving	Humble
Entrepreneurial	Gritty	Modest
Enthusiastic	Bold	Prudent
Trustworthy	Grateful	Spiritual
Honest	Appreciative	Mindful
Engaged		

Select the words that mean the most to your family and write them down. Try to limit it to no more than ten values.

A family once came to me with a beautiful drawing of about 200 values all broken down into categories. A consultant had helped them come up with this list. The daughter said, "This looks really pretty." She pointed to a little drawing of a boat next to values that represented fun and family bonding. "But," she said, "there's just too many of them. We have no idea what our family represents!" Don't make this mistake. Too many values dilutes focus. Prioritize your values.

Your Mantra

Your mantra needs to be a catchy, memorable statement that sticks in your head. You may have only one for your family, or you may have a few. But stop at three short mantras; too many can water down the message.

To start developing your mantra, ask your family members, "What sayings best capture our family?" You can look to quote books, poems, or famous speeches, or make up something. Have everyone throw out ideas and select the top phrases.

Some examples include:

- My actions matter, whether others see them or not.

- Question authority.

- Always ask why.

- Is there a better way?

- We take the road less traveled. (Inspired by Robert Frost and M. Scott Peck.)

- Families who play together stay together.

- The means are just as important as the ends.

- Follow your bliss. (Courtesy of Joseph Campbell.)

- Honor the family name.

- We are spiritual beings having a human experience.

- What would Jesus do?

- This little light of mine, I'm gonna let it shine! (Courtesy of Avis Burgeson Christiansen.)

- Don't hide your candle under a bushel. (Biblical reference.)

- We were born to manifest the glory of God within us. (Courtesy of Marianne Williamson and Nelson Mandela.)

- Nothing great was ever achieved without enthusiasm! (Courtesy of Ralph Waldo Emerson.)

- Carpe diem! (Courtesy of Horace.)

- Never look back.

- Pay it forward.

- Follow your gut.

- Stay curious.

- No empty chairs.

- A quick wrong decision is better than indecision.

- It's okay to make mistakes.

- We dream "impossible" dreams.

- We are travelers, not tourists.

- We bring others together.

- We are always looking for the good in others.

- We push through with faith!

- There is a solution to every problem.

Your mantra is important because it keeps the family aligned. Just as when a sports team has a particular chant that brings hope and encouragement, your mantra represents the essence of your family's spirit and goals. Repeating it to each other on a regular basis bonds you together.

Your Family Mission

Once you've identified what's important to your family, your values, and your mantra, it's time to write out a longer statement about your purpose. A few things to keep in mind are:

- Keep it short: Short is easy to remember. You want a meaningful mission statement that resonates. Try to keep it under one hundred words. (Although, there is an example of longer statement coming up that one of my colleagues found effective.)

- Collaborate: Ask each family member to write two or three sentences incorporating some of your family's top values. Discuss with each other the meaning of these sentences, what works, and what could be adapted or changed.

- Take your time: Write, edit, and rewrite as much as necessary. Remember, this statement will guide your family for years to come, so take the time to get it right.

See the following examples to get an idea of what a family mission statement looks like.

Shorter anonymous mission statements:

To support, respect, and love each other in good times and bad so that we are happy, and fulfilled, and know that we always have someone in our corner.

To honor each other's unique abilities, make each other laugh, push each other to grow, and give openly to our friends and neighbors.

The mission of our family is to create a nurturing place of order, love, happiness, and relaxation, and to pro-

vide opportunities for each person to become respon-sibly independent and effectively interdependent, in order to achieve worthwhile purposes.

From Stephen Covey's *The 7 Habits of Highly Effective Families*:

Our family mission is to:

Value honesty with ourselves and others.

Create an environment where each of us can find support and encouragement in achieving our life's goals.

Respect and accept each person's unique personality and talents.

Promote a loving, kind, and happy atmosphere.

Support family endeavors that better society.

Maintain patience through understanding.

Always resolve conflicts with each other rather than harboring anger.

Promote the realization of life's treasures.

The Feiler[25] family mission statement (drafted with input from the author's five-year-old):

May our first word be adventure and our last word be love.

We live lives of passion.

---

25 Author of *The Secrets of Happy Families*.

We dream un-dreamable dreams.

We are travelers, not tourists.

We help others to fly.

We love to learn.

We don't like dilemmas, we like solutions.

We push through. We believe!

We know it's okay to make mistakes.

We bring people together.

We are joy, rapture, yay!

The McKay[26] family mission statement:

We love and serve God.

We strive to make our home a refuge from the cares and troubles of the world.

We do hard things.

We're creators, not consumers.

We stay hungry and humble.

We face adversity with stoicism.

We show kindness to our family members and others.

We help each other reach our potential.

We're devoted to lifelong learning.

---

26 Brett and Kate McKay, www.artofmanliness.com.

We know that sacrifice brings forth the blessings of Heaven.

We face life with a sense of humor and a lot of laughter.

The Diefendorf[27] family mission statement:

As a family, nuclear and extended, we see to be unified as a unit so that we can be a powerful force to impact our world in a meaningful way. We will share the gift of prayer by actively participating in petitioning God on behalf of each family member. We will live out our family values and encourage each other when we fall. It is our goal to live intentionally, making the best of each and every day, as we know they are numbered here on Earth. And ultimately, we will seek to glorify God in ALL that we do.

This is a longer statement one of my colleagues, attorney Michael Stuart of Wojcicki Law, who was kind enough to share with me:

It is our hope that this statement of our collective vision as a family will endure and give guidance to our family for many generations and encourage the members of our family to live productive lives in harmony with our values. Our family, our environment and our priorities focus on developing the following qualities in each family member:

> *Excellence*
>
> *Thoughtfulness and compassion*

---

27 Provided by Monroe M. Diefendorf, Jr., CEO of 3 Dimensional Wealth Advisory.

Honesty

Humility

Patience

Spirituality

Personal

Each person is encouraged to develop his (or her) own interests and talents; to "follow his own muse." Education, love of reading, and lifetime learning have served us well over time and are fully supported. We recognize the importance of art, music, and travel in ensuring that we are well-rounded, informed individuals. Everyone is supported in developing a career that is challenging, rewarding, and that they love. We are all supported in developing other interests (hobbies). We stress the importance of healthy living, exercise, personal private time, and nutrition. Thrift and savings are taught and encouraged. Each family member strives to become more organized, to develop patience, and perseverance, and to "never give up." Everyone has high expectations for themselves and each other, and we support each other in those endeavors. We encourage the development of a balanced life. Everyone is responsible for his or her own actions.

As a family, we revere admirable characteristics in others, such as being committed, enthusiastic, industrious, creative, educated, and sensitive, and attempt to implement similar characteristics in our own lives.

Each member of our family is encouraged and supported in their journey to become educated, responsible, sensitive, balanced, patient, organized, loyal, self-reliant, wise, compassionate, and selfless in their lives.

Social

Family and friends are extremely important priorities. We respect others, elders, and the environment. A home structure is maintained that helps develop each family member into a thoughtful, productive member of society. Each of us has an obligation to give back to our community with our time and our monetary giving.

Spiritual

We support each other in our own spiritual journeys. We recognize the importance of a spiritual focus in our lives. We strive to find our individual spirituality inside of us daily. We try to live our lives with the "Open Heart of Compassion."

We will try to incorporate this mission statement into our daily lives and encourage our family members to do so as well.

Many people go back to the values they learned from being a part of clubs, religions, or organizations. Is there anything from these famous organizations you can apply to your family?

Scout oath:

On my honor, I will do my best

To do my duty to God and my country and to obey the Scout Law;

To help other people at all times;

To keep myself physically strong, mentally awake and morally straight.

Rotary 4-Way Test:

Of the things we think, say or do:

1. *Is it the TRUTH?*

2. *Is it FAIR to all concerned?*

3. *Will it build GOODWILL and BETTER FRIEND-SHIPS?*

4. *Will it be BENEFICIAL to all concerned?*

Family Rules

Family rules: a body of principles or established precedents that a family acknowledges to be governed.

Imagine showing up at school for the first time. You walk into the classroom and sit in an empty chair. The teacher scolds you for sitting in the wrong seat.

"But I didn't know I wasn't supposed to sit here," you protest.

She glares at you as you move to the chair she points at. Then she sighs as you put your book on the desk. "Blue books are not allowed on Mondays," she says.

"I'm sorry. I didn't know."

"Is that a green pen?" she asks, pointing to the writing instrument in your hand.

"Yes."

"Go to the principal's office. I can't deal with you!"

"But . . . I didn't know I was breaking the rules. Is there some sort of rule book or list of guidelines?" you ask.

"No!" she barks. "You should already know this stuff! Now go!"

This is how a lot of parents handle their children. There are rules—moral and behavioral guidelines—in the parents' heads, but they are not spelled out for the children up front. It's a brutal way to learn what is and isn't appropriate, and kids start feeling like they're constantly walking on eggshells.

If there is a set of principles that governs your family, it not only makes life easier but also gives each family member a set of metrics by which to gauge his or her behavior.

It's about Action

If your family mission, values, and mantra is your broad expression of intent, then your family rules are your set of guidelines to achieve your mission.

Keep your family rules short and to the point. The idea is to have a document that outlines how you will treat each other and operate on a daily basis. If you have significant assets and need a governance structure to manage the family business, investments, or real estate holdings, this is too simplified for that. You'll want to bring in an advisory firm that specializes in family governance and is intimately familiar with your financial assets and goals.

The purpose of your family rules is to keep your family functioning well and focused on what's important despite busy schedules, catastrophes, arguments, less-than-ideal situations, and all the other distractions that can knock us off course.

Your family rules should contain the following elements:

1. Behavior. What actions are expected to keep things orderly?

2. Communication. How should family members address each other and resolve conflicts?

3. Fit on one page. For your rules to work, they must be easy to understand and follow. Make them as simple as possible.

A Few Examples of Family Rules

House Rules

1. Empty containers don't go in the refrigerator.

2. Pick up your own mess. (And don't clutter!)

3. Always use coasters.

4. No shouting across the house.

5. Never steal the last cookie.

6. No talking when someone else is talking.

7. Wash your hands before dinner.

Our Family Rules

1. Always tell the truth.

2. Say I love you.

3. Keep your promises.

4. Don't blame.

5. Use kind words.

6. Do your best.

7. Learn from your mistakes.

8. Say please and thank you.

9. Be grateful.

10. Forgive and forget.

Family Commandments

1. Thou shalt be in bed by 11:00 p.m.

2. Thou shalt not bring thy smartphone to family dinner.

3. Thou shalt not badmouth thy family to outsiders.

4. Thou shalt be accountable and follow through.

5. Thou shalt take a timeout when thou art fuming mad and may say something regretful.

6. Thou shalt treat thy family and friends better than thou expects in return.

7. Thou shalt talk about thy feelings of frustration early on and not bottle them.

8. Thou shalt support thy family members' decisions.

9. Thou shalt work hard and finish thy chores before play.

10. Thou shalt say what thou art grateful for before complaining.

Communication Guidelines

1. All participants have an equal voice.

2. No eye rolls allowed.

3. No decisions made in a crisis.

4. No drama triangles.

5. No justifications or blaming.

6. Listen before you speak.

7. Tell the truth about how you're feeling.

8. We don't argue—we negotiate.

Coat of Arms

The original intention of a coat of arms was to distinguish military commanders from common soldiers. Men were often masked by metal helmets and quickly became unrecognizable in the thick of battle. A unique coat of arms identified each commander, the symbols representing characteristics of his family or bravery. Eventually, these effigies transcended their military distinctions to become short history pieces on valor and family achievement.

Why Your Family Should Have Its Own Coat of Arms

A coat of arms or logo gives your family a tangible identity—something they can see and connect with. The coat of arms represents your family's successes and values while maintaining a connection with the generations that preceded it. Although a coat of arms cannot capture every ideal and happy achievement, it commands a certain air of awe and respect. Because its origins are rooted in royalty and honor, the coat of arms represents high morals of love and dignity that accompany a strong family legacy.

If you come from European descent, you could simply use the coat of arms that represents your family name, but I recommend creating your own that aligns with your specific family legacy right now. If a coat of arms seems too formal or traditional for your family, consider a logo or another symbol that represents what you are trying to accomplish.

Creating Your Own Coat of Arms

Creating your own coat of arms can be a rewarding experience for you and your family. Unless you want an official coat of arms and are willing to go through the proper channels (such as the College of Arms in London), this type of exercise doesn't have to be restrictive. You can add or omit as many elements as you wish. The purpose is not to have something "official" but instead to represent your family's values.

You can work with an artist to bring your vision to life, or your family members can design it themselves. My company has experts that specialize in the creation of a coat of arms—both the graphical components and the meaning behind them. But you don't need a whole creative team—create your own by following some simple steps.

Visit **www.meaninglegacytools.com** to access information about designing your own coat of arms.

6

Master Stories
Your Stories Change Lives

---

*"Stories have to be told or they die, and when they die, we can't
remember who we are or why we're here."*
—Sue Monk Kidd, American writer

Oral storytelling has been the foundation of passing on legacy since the beginning of human language. It is how cultures
maintained their traditions and taught new generations wisdom from the past. You can tell your children to have integrity or to be kind and loving, but these abstract concepts have
very little impact unless they are accompanied by an experience. Stories are one of the most profound ways to connect
with emotions and teach lessons that will be remembered for
a lifetime.

You may never publish a memoir for the public to see, and
there certainly are reasons to keep your life private, but withholding your wisdom from your loved ones is like watching
them try to catch fish with a wooden bat. If only you had tak-

en five minutes to explain that they need a fishing pole with the proper line and bait, then they'd be much further ahead. Sure, they may have figured this out on their own—after lots of trial and error—but why not give them the ability to start at a much higher level and use their time more productively? Your stories are a resource for living and learning.

The Power of Family Storytelling

My brother and I were born about two years apart. We have the same parents, went to the same schools, sat around the same dinner table, and watched the same shows. I always thought our childhood was pretty much the same, until, as adults, he started sharing his perspective with me. He told me how my parents treated him growing up, his thoughts about the religion we were raised in, and his feelings about our heritage—most of what he said I had never even considered. As he explained his views, I thought, *Am I delusional? How did I miss all of this?*

Stories are not fact. They depend entirely on the values, perspective, and memory of the one telling the story. A story reveals much more about the one telling the story than it does about a specific event.

Storytelling is a tool to build community and bring families closer together. There've been several studies showing the positive impacts family storytelling has on children's sense of self, social skills, and ability to navigate life. There's a healing aspect to stories as well. James Birren, one of the founders of the field of gerontology, discovered in his guided autobiography work that when seniors share their stories, they have reduced rates of depression and anxiety. This kind of storytelling has also been known to improve cognitive function, reduce chronic pain, and further personal growth and self-discovery.

But it's not just cathartic for the one telling the story. A good story can also heal families and patch up wounds of the past.

Here's a simple example of how quickly your perspective can change: Let's say you're driving your car to work, and the car in front of you stops. There's no red light and hence no reason to stop. After a few seconds, you lay on your horn. The car still doesn't move. Now you are fuming. Who is this moron who isn't paying attention? You get out of your car and walk toward the stopped vehicle, screaming profanities— until you see a pregnant woman in the back seat. She's in labor, and the driver is trying to help her. Immediately, your point of view changes. The story you had in your head about a selfish, lazy, incompetent driver evaporates, and you immediately experience compassion for the couple.

Understanding the inner workings of why people behave the way they do can bring forgiveness, significance, and love. When you understand why your father drank, the sacrifices your grandmother made to start the family business, or why your brother is paranoid about spending money, it provides an opportunity to see things from their eyes and connect.

The Novel of Your Life

It can be tough to look back and pick out plot points that have composed the novel of your life—especially if you haven't reached an advanced age or don't have enough perspective to see the inner workings of your own personal novel yet.

But there are strategies to bring out these points and keep refining your personal novel, now and in the future—no matter your age or stage in life. You want the highlights. You want the wisdom you attained. You want the lessons you learned. You want to pass on the best parts of yourself.

Questions to Add Perspective

You may not always know what's important as you're going through an experience, but adding some perspective-enhancing questions will help with the process. As far as what you do with the information after you've asked the questions is up to you, but I'd recommend keeping a journal, posting it on a website that makes it easy to archive and save your most important memories, or turning it into a video or book.

When you're archiving memories, you'll want to look at the distant past, the not-so-distant past, and the current time.

Distant Past Questions

The distant past is typically easier to put into perspective. Here's some questions to get you started:

1. What was growing up like for you?

2. What have been the best times of your life so far? Why were they meaningful?

3. What have been the best learning experiences so far?

4. Who are the most impactful people in your life and why?

5. What are your most cherished family memories?

Not-So-Distant Past Questions

Consider what has happened to you over the last year and think about these questions:

1. What is the most significant thing that has happened in my life over the past year?

2. What stage am I at in my life, and how is that impacting my viewpoints?

3. What seemed important to me a few months ago that is no longer important? (You probably won't archive this, but it will get you to start filtering events with a higher level of awareness as they happen.)

Current Events Questions

These are questions to ask as you're going through an experience:

1. In a hundred years, when someone is reading about me, will this memory matter? (This one's tricky, because what seems trivial—like how sweet the flowers smell when you walk to visit your lover—could seem insignificant now but may be a beautiful detail when you talk about visiting your husband-to-be in the future.)

2. How can I make the most of what's happening right now (e.g., a vacation, a hike, going to school, or other event)? What significance does it have?

Not every event needs to have significance—and you don't need to manufacture it. But there are times when everything seems to click. Like when you're around a table with your friends, laughing and joking, and the night unfolds in a magical way. Or when the opposite happens—when you're on your way to work, you get a flat tire, the tow truck is two hours late, and someone helps you on the side of the road and changes your outlook. When you find yourself in these moments, take time to record your feelings and insights.

It's these small moments of reflection that make up the novel of your life. Your life's novel, however, isn't significant because of the events that took place. It's significant because of how you interpreted those events and what choices they led to.

Passing on Wisdom and Love

After journaling about your stories, consider your audience. Who are the stories for? It's no problem if they're only for yourself (after all, Marcus Aurelius wrote his *Meditations* to help himself analyze his character). But if you want to pass on your stories to your children, grandchildren, or others, think through what will be the most interesting and valuable to them.

A general rule of thumb is that you want to pass on stories that had the most significant impact in your own life—times you learned a valuable lesson, experienced extreme joy, or saw a situation from a different angle. Not every story needs to be a great parable to pass on wisdom. Stories can be fun too: your most-embarrassing moments or quirky behaviors of family members. Silly stories can bond you to people the same way a nickname or an inside joke does.

Are there some stories you're worried about passing on? If so, don't tell a story if:

1. It's inappropriate for its audience (i.e. has swearing or adult topics when little kids will be listening).

2. It's not empowering, or it turns you into a victim, and there's no lesson or redemption at the end.

3. It spreads misery (i.e., the whole point is to get revenge or slander someone).

4. It uses blame or justification.

5. It betrays someone by disclosing private details that you'd promised to keep secret.

6. It isn't the truth.

Don't let this list scare you, though. Most stories can be passed on. There's a tendency to be concerned about how a certain story will affect someone in the family, but often if you run it by them before you share it or clarify that the story is from your perspective, it goes over well.

When you come up with a story, consider its universal theme. If the principles can't be applied to a wider audience, it loses its appeal.

According to a study done by Microsoft, the average attention span of a human is eight seconds. (The average attention span of goldfish is nine seconds.) Thanks to our digital world, everyone is constantly distracted and their attention must be hooked within eight seconds—or they move on to something else.

In order for stories to hold the attention of those listening, they must be engaging and applicable. This means you need to mold your memories into stories that are short, specific, and unique, and they must convey a message without being overly preachy. It's an art, but it's one that can be taught and isn't all that hard once you know the structure.

Expanding Beyond Yourself to Capture Family Stories

My favorite method for capturing family stories is the formal interview, which is different than an ordinary conversation. It's more specific and focused on gathering information about your interviewee's life. If you want to be sure your mother's stories are recorded, don't wait for her to spring to action and whip out a memoir—it's too easy for her to put it off. Plus, much of the benefit of recording her stories is interacting with her. If you have children, you could also get them involved.

Record the interview via audio or video. I teach an entire online course about how to capture and craft family stories, and every aspect matters, from the pre-interview to the questions you ask to the kind of equipment you use to the way you map out each story. I recommend going through specific questions to take someone through a step-by-step retelling of their master stories or experiences during a specific time period. This way, it's much easier to mold the answers into a coherent narrative rather than working with a smattering of memory fragments.

The formal interview gives you a sense of openness that's hard to come by in normal life. When you can sit with a family member and ask questions you never dared to ask in the past, it can be liberating for both parties.

When I was growing up, for example, my dad always acted

funny about me going on dates or meeting boys, and so I just shut off those kinds of conversations with him. But as I got older, I began interviewing him and asking him questions about what dating was like for him growing up. I was taken aback by how honest he was; it didn't feel awkward at all.

The kind of bonding and understanding that can develop from these interviews is truly a gift for yourself and your loved ones, but expect some resistance. Opening up and talking about yourself can be intimidating. Many people are insecure about being on camera or having their voices recorded.

One of the first photo shoots I ever did at my marketing company was for a client who had consulted with hundreds of people in her business. She was vivacious, charismatic, gorgeous, and personable. But once I put her in front of the camera, her posture changed. She folded her arms, shrinking into herself. Her cheeks went red with embarrassment.

"What's wrong?" I asked.

"I just hate cameras," she said. I tried coaching her through it, but I couldn't get her to smile naturally or loosen up. Over the years, I've gotten better at helping people feel comfortable, but you never know how certain people will respond to your request to interview them. Sometimes it's hard to be in the spotlight.

Before the interview, go through the topics with your subject and plan how you're going to shape the content. A structured approach gives your family stories purpose, and helps your loved ones go beyond reporting surface details.

A successful project often comes down to how well the interviewer listens and highlights communication strengths of their interviewee and then compiles the captured audio or video into a format that is entertaining.

Top Five Stories Your Children Need to Know

The following are the top five categories of stories your children should know. Your goal is always to create a positive, continuing dialogue with your children, and these stories will get the conversation started. You can tell these stories casually or more formally, but at some point, take the time to record them either via writing, video, or audio. One day, your family will appreciate having your stories archived. Hearing your voice or seeing your face and mannerisms adds another element they will treasure.

Story Category 1: Life Before Them

Your children need to know how their parents met, what it was like for you growing up, and early memories you have about your childhood, teen years, what school you went to, etc.

Story Category 2: Their History

Your children need to know about each side of their family tree—their grandparents, great-grandparents, and anything you can tell them about where they came from. Why did you pick their name? What significance does it have? What was it like in the hospital when they were born?

Story Category 3: The Tough Times

Explain to your children about difficult times your family members have experienced. Tell them about your personal struggles and how you persevered. This will give them a sense that they can persevere as well.

Story Category 4: The Happy Times

Tell your children about what makes you happy—your greatest loves, your passions, people you've loved, and goals you've striven for and accomplished.

Story Category 5: Lessons to Live By

If you could only give your children a handful of principles to guide their lives, what would those be in short, concise statements? Now think of a story to illustrate each principle and tell the story to reinforce it.

*Visit **www.meaninglegacytools.com** to download our Story Arc worksheet and tips about how to collect family stories.*

7

Experiential Bonds

Culture of the Family

"Ritual is important to us as human beings. It ties us to our traditions and our histories."

—Miller Williams, American contemporary poet

When adults are asked what they remember most from childhood, they often describe rituals or family traditions that made them feel part of something bigger and secure. That exhausted yet peaceful feeling driving back from a weekend together at the cottage. The sheer joy of crazy dancing on the beach with Mum and Dad, roasting marshmallows or piling up wood for the bonfire. These memories are what make us positive and happier adults.

Webster's Dictionary defines culture as "the integrated pattern of human knowledge, belief, and behavior that depends upon the capacity for learning and transmitting knowledge to succeeding generations." The word "culture" is from the Latin *colere*, which means to tend, to grow, to cultivate, and to nurture. Most people associate culture with a certain country or ethnic group, but the family unit is its own culture. We are all defined by the culture in which we live, and this begins at home.

Although the concept of "family" is quickly changing, for those who had ancestors who migrated to Northern America several generations back, our family culture tends to be a Westernized version that over the years has become the norm for us. The nuclear family unit is a direct result of years of emigration to the new world and separation from our families and communities through these passages to a new environment.

Culture used to be considered somewhat static and essentially a compilation of values and beliefs that were established to guide a group of individuals to becoming a community. Research, however, has shown that culture is not static. Author of *The Cultural Nature of Human Development* Nancy Rogoff states that, "In my view, human development is a process in which people transform through their ongoing participation in cultural activities, which in turn contribute to changes in their cultural communities across generations."

Cultural traditions are what bind us to the past, but those bindings are not immutable. We can change, adapt, and adjust those traditions as the family requires. Birth, death, marriage, and divorce change the family in profound ways. Families, like societies, are in constant transition, and the economic and political climate will have an impact on the family unit. History and time changes many things, including the definition of a family, from social revolution to attitudes and expectations about gender roles, women in the workplace, and so on. We can move traditions from ancient history to current moments and adapt them to what works for us in different times.

Throughout history, when family members all lived in one place, their traditions became the foundations of family life. These traditions were kept alive by the family elders and built into the daily life of the whole family. As the years went by and families began to separate and become smaller, traditions began to die out, but many families kept some old traditions alive because it helped them feel connected to their family, even though oceans separated them.

Even family members who have rejected or moved away from their family of origin often find themselves repeating traditions from childhood. Regardless of how much they want to separate from the family culture or disavow certain attitudes, some traditions are so deeply ingrained that they become a part of us.

Creating Family Traditions

Creating family traditions and rituals doesn't have to be difficult or time-consuming. Many of us already have traditions that have been passed down from generation to generation, even though we may have forgotten the original source.

You probably already have several traditions you follow with your family on holidays or special occasions. In England, it's traditional on November 11 to "burn the guy" on a massive community bonfire. This harks back to the day when Guy Fawkes got caught trying to blow up the houses of Parliament. In Ireland, many Irish take the pilgrims' walk up Croagh Patrick in honor of St. Patrick. At a Swedish wedding, it is traditional for the bride and groom to walk down the aisle together—nobody has to "give them away." In Japan, it is traditional to eat ehomaki sushi rolls in February. This ritual involves eating an entire roll of sushi (uncut) while facing a lucky direction, and this must be done in complete silence.

By learning about your family traditions and rituals, you can preserve them, pass them on to future generations, and keep strong ties to your heritage. There are several ways to establish family traditions. Here are a handful:

- Family events: game night, reunions, vacations, or holidays

- Special meals: Sunday morning brunch, a monthly visit to Grandma's house for homemade pies and pot roast, pizza night

- Daily routines: a book before bedtime, family dinnertime

- Family calls: Skyping or calling family members or siblings away from home

- Recreational activities: family hikes, walks, sports, or other activities

- Holidays: from food served to rituals and traditions observed within the family

- Rituals or celebrations: christenings, weddings, or coming-of-age parties

- Celebrations: birthdays, the first day of school, graduations, prom nights, or first sleepover

Uncovering Old Family Traditions

Teach your children how to learn about their family history.

Have them ask the elders in the family what their traditions are. When you have family gatherings, encourage the children to visit with older folks and listen to their stories.

Bonding through Traditions

Traditions of all sizes and types are important in that they create strong bonds between family members. As your children get older, the memories you create with them become their traditions and something to share with their future family. Meg Cox's book, *New Family Traditions*, suggests that there are three types of traditions every family should have. She breaks them into these categories:

- **Daily Connection Traditions**, which are the small things families do every day. They can be routines such as bedtime stories, daily walks or family dinners.

- **Weekly Connection Traditions** are similar to Daily Connection Traditions but involve a special activity or ritual that your family looks forward to each week. This could be a family Sunday brunch, a walk in the park and a picnic, or a family game night.

- **Life Changes Traditions** are a way to celebrate the big things in life, changes such as a new job or school, children leaving home for college or travel, births, weddings, or other milestones in the family's life. These traditions can be something as simple as taking a yearly first-day-of-school picture or something more profound, like dedicating a new home.

Being Choosy

If you want to create a new family tradition, first ask, "What is the purpose of this new tradition? What will my family get out of it?" You don't want so many traditions that your family feels like every vacation or dinnertime is a scheduled performance. Your traditions will average out in their heads; if there are too many, nothing will stick out as particularly memorable.

I also don't want to oversell traditions. Some of the greatest memories involve spontaneity. Do you have to go to the same restaurant year after year on your family vacation? Maybe exploring new spots to eat would be a healthy change.

Don't create tradition simply for the sake of it. It'll turn you into a narrow-minded family who must always do things the same way. Make sure your traditions are meaningful, enjoyed by your family, and scarce enough that they truly are special.

Anatomy of a Family Retreat

Many families hold events or retreats as a way to pass on values and to bond. If you haven't created your family identity (as outlined in Chapter 5) yet, a family retreat could be the perfect forum to come up with your mission, values, mantra and coat of arms.

In addition to planning fun activities—such as sightseeing, dinners or game nights—a family retreat has an added layer of depth when you include components to educate family members. Let's review the elements needed to craft an effective family retreat:

1. **Theme:** Determine what the event is focused on. Some examples of themes include "Health", "Philanthropic Giving" or "Learning About Money."

2. **Purpose(s)**: State why you are holding the event, what you expect your family to learn and why the theme is important.

3. **Preparation**: What does your family need to do to prepare for the event? Do they need to read certain books, prepare a topic to present or watch a video?

4. **Agenda / List of Activities**: Compose a scheduled list of activities for each day.

Example Agenda

The following is an example agenda outlining the activities for one day of a family retreat. Ideally, you will have three to four days with various outings, games, projects, educational discussions or challenges for your family to participate in.

DAY 1: Hopper Family Retreat

Theme: Mindful Living

Purposes:

1. To learn more about being mindful.

2. To update each other about major accomplishments in our lives.

3. To review the latest happenings in the family and have a reminder of our principles.

Preparation:

1. Read *Mindfulness in Plain English* by Bhante Henepola Gunaratana.

2. Review letter from Grandpa about updates.

Assigned Topics:

- Melinda: Meditation

- Tony: Health and Wellness

- Becky: Financial Mindfulness

- Grandma Grace: Family Stories about Triumph

- Grandpa Jack: State of the Family

Agenda/List of Activities:

8:00-9:00	Breakfast / Notes of Appreciation
9:00-9:30	Guided Meditation (Melinda)
9:30-10:30	Health and Wellness (Tony)
10:30-11:30	Financial Mindfulness Game (Becky)
12:00-1:00	Lunch - Stories (Grandpa & Grandma)
1:00-2:00	State of the Family Address (Grandpa)
2:00-3:30	Waterfall Hike
3:30-4:00	Snacks
4:00-5:30	Break
5:30-7:00	Dinner
7:00-9:00	Life Updates and Celebrations
9:30-10:30	Songs Around the Fire Pit

Things to Remember:

- Gratitude Rule in effect.

- Health Goal: Walk at least 10,000 steps – top walker gets a new iPad!

- To Accomplish Before End of the Retreat: 1) Everyone has their personal goals written up for the coming year and 2) write favorite memory over the last 12 months.

You can see how a few days like this could serve to unite the family and educate family members in a fun way. In the next chapter, we'll review how to add even more depth to your legacy by researching your family history.

8

Family Heritage
Tracking Your Roots

"A people's relationship to their heritage is the same as the relationship of a child to its mother."

—John Henrik Clarke, African American historian and professor

Thanks to the ease at which information can now be cataloged, advancements in DNA testing, the popularity of several genealogy platforms, and reality TV shows like *Find My Past*, family history is a rising trend. The average personal history enthusiast spends between $1,000 to $18,000 per year to discover his or her roots.[28]

In this chapter, we'll cover the basics of family history and what you need to know. Understanding where you came from and what your family represents is important. When children know about their past, they feel more confident and like they

---

28 According to studies provided by Global Industry Analysts, Inc. (http://www.prweb.com/releases/genealogy_research/ancestors_archives/prweb9092131.htm).

belong to something greater. The more you can help them to see how their presence fits into your family tree, the more they feel they are a part of something special.

What You Should Know

The following is a brief outline of what you should know about your family history.

Personal History

Archive where you were born as well as important milestones in your life—such as getting married or graduating from college; significant memories about your parents, siblings, children, and other relatives; and your thoughts about life and your journey through it. Think of yourself as a historian who is documenting important dates and facts.

Family Tree

You can use a service like ancestry.com or familysearch.org to research both sides of your family and map out your family tree. Try to go at least three generations back, and do a little research to find out if any people in your family were famous or had interesting stories published in newspapers. Imagine finding out that your great-grandmother was one of the first female doctors, your great-great-grandfather fought at Gettysburg, or your family is related to royalty. If your family immigrated at some point, try to go back to at least as far as where they originally came from.

Memories, Photos, and Records of Ancestors

Do you have old videotapes of family members? What about photos, slides, or negatives? Make sure these memories are converted into a digital format so that you can save and share them. Also, add them to a physical book or print them. There are a variety of services that will convert your photos and videos. Some require you to organize them, box them up, and send them in. Others send someone to your home to scan your photos in real time.

Cultural Heritage

Find out what kinds of cultural influences shaped your family. This fits in with rituals and traditions. Are there recipes you should archive? What about certain clothing your family used to wear? Or places they used to visit or live?

DNA Makeup

The number of companies popping up in the DNA analysis realm is astounding. I'm amazed at how much progress has been made in just a few short years. I suspect that anything I write about DNA analysis and its relation to ancestry will be obsolete by the time it's read, but on a very basic level, you want to see where your DNA leads you. The amount of information you can learn about your cultural and health background is mind-blowing. And it's now quite affordable to have your DNA tested.

A small part of me is a little paranoid about privacy issues with these third-party companies, but I got over it and now have pretty charts outlining what percentage of Irish and

Scandinavian is in my genes. If you worry about privacy and aren't ready to make the jump to having your DNA cataloged, I understand—Gattaca may be closer than we think.

Descendant Connections

Not too long ago, a distant cousin reached out to me on a website that I tested my DNA through. We chatted a bit and formed an instant connection. We now have a standing invitation to have lunch the next time either one of us is visiting each other's town. Since then, I've reached out to more previously unknown relatives and have received similar responses.

Cultivating relationships with cousins, aunts, and uncles— even ones who are far removed—can be incredibly rewarding, and for some mysterious reason, there's something innate about blood relations sticking together. You instantly have an interest in them and want to support them. It's not a bad idea to start building up that support system, and DNA and ancestry sites make it easy to make those connections.

Where to Start

Before you begin your own research, talk with your relatives. You may discover that a cousin or your aunt has completed much of the family tree. In my family, there are a variety of family history enthusiasts on both sides. Ask your family about physical items too, such as photos, the family Bible, family letters, or journals. You may need to go beyond who you know well. Distant cousins can be a great resource for this kind of work.

Be consistent and organized. Don't jumble everything together in a folder. It's easy to become inundated with too much information. Have some sort of summary for each relative, such as a document that lists each person's date of birth, death, marriage, and any interesting details you can find about them.

Many experts recommend working on one generation at a time—starting with the most recent and working backward. You can also take a shotgun approach: Pull information in when you find it and then methodically fill in the holes after the fact. This approach works for smaller families. If your family is large, however, the generation-by-generation method will keep your research manageable.

Like any good detective work, family history research is part luck, part skill, and part persistence. You never know what random details could lead to; maybe you find your great-great-great-grandmother's name next to a man's name on a wedding invitation from another family member, and that's how you discover whom she was married to. If you don't want to conduct family history research on your own, you can always find an experienced family historian to coach you through the process or do the research for you.

There are a variety of websites to get you started. I'd recommend checking these out first:

Basic Family Search Sites

www.ancestry.com — with 2.7 million subscribers, the largest commercial genealogy website; also available free through many libraries

www.familysearch.org — the genealogy site of the LDS-run Family History Library

Family Records

www.archives.com — Quickly and simply search more than 4.8 billion photos, newspapers, and vital records to get information about your ancestors

www.ellisisland.org — 25 million immigrant arrival records available free online

www.findmypast.com — an online archive of over 2 billion historical records from around the world

Genealogy through Social Media

www.cyndislist.com/social-networking — a nice gathering of sites and resources

www.genforum.genealogy.com/ — Genealogy.com's social media site

www.rootsweb.ancestry.com/ — Ancestry.com's social media site

DNA Testing

www.23andme.com — one of the top DNA testing sites for health and ancestry information

www.ancestry.com/dna/ — Ancestry.com's DNA testing site

Family history websites have gotten so good at collecting and sorting data from the past that you may be surprised by what you can learn about your family after spending just a few hours researching your lineage.

9

Community Impact
Giving with Meaning

"Philanthropy and social change work are at their best when they are driven by your values and connected to what you care about most."
—Charles Bronfman, Canadian / American businessman and philanthropist

When I spoke with Sierra Visher Kroha, executive director for San Diego Social Venture Partners, she said something that has stuck with me about the definition of philanthropy: "I used to think of philanthropists only as people who give their money. You know, you have so much wealth to give away and that qualifies you for the space, but I've been learning over the last few years that the majority of philanthropists and actors in the social change community really think of philanthropists as anyone who is giving themselves or their time or their heart and soul to a social cause, and it has nothing to do with the money."

In this chapter, we'll discuss how to craft your philanthropic mission and get involved in something you care about at a profound level. I'll also review how to get your family involved. Charity work is one of the most powerful ways to teach humility, love, and responsibility to children (and adults, for that matter).

Different motivations drive different people. For our magazine, I've interviewed a variety of people from varying backgrounds, and everyone has their own take on how they give back to the world.

I've found, however, that there are common drivers depending on someone's personality. As you read through the giving personalities, think about what resonates with you. On a fundamental level, giving back and connecting with others is something we need, but we don't all get that connection in the same way. You don't have to follow a rigid path of giving. There are many different flavors—do what fits your personality.

Top Seven Giving Personalities

Mentor/Succession Planner

Mentors or succession planners are interested in passing the baton to the next generation or training those who ask for help. They love to spread their knowledge to help others become more successful and competent. This could mean mentoring people in a business or teaching certain skills (such as how to paint, balance a budget, or surf).

Kindness Spreader

The goal of kindness spreaders is to make others feel good. They are always there with a kind word or encouraging comment. They may regularly bring donuts into work, visit their neighbors, or be the one their friends call when they need someone to talk to. They're always there to listen or give a hug. They are the peacemakers and hate contention. They regularly reach out to others and enjoy one-on-one connection.

Crisis Reliever

Crisis relievers want to help people (or animals) who are going through a rough patch. When something bad happens in the community or a neighbor's basement floods, they are the first ones there to help. They also may volunteer at the hospital to work with terminally ill patients, take in foster kids, or travel to other countries to give medical procedures to those in need.

Cultural Enthusiast

These are people who love the arts: music, fine art, writing, theater, and so on. They see the value of contributing to a gallery or modern dance project. It is in connecting with creative people and their visions that they gain understanding. They want others to have this connection and want to support artists in making the world a more beautiful, thoughtful place.

Infrastructure Enhancer

These are individuals who want to improve the infrastructure within their communities or outside of them (such as Brad Pitt working with the charity Make It Right to build homes in New Orleans). They contribute to schools, universities, libraries, hospitals, building restorations, and community projects. Rockefeller was extremely influential in this area; his family foundation still is. Many public buildings are the result of his contributions and those of others like him.

Change Agent

Change agents see a problem and are determined to change it. This can be done as a part of a group or as a vision they pursue on their own. They may want to end animal abuse, create a program to help veterans deal with depression, fix the healthcare system, educate immigrants, save trees in South America, or teach kids resilience. There is an issue that irritates them, and they're out to make it better. Sometimes, this takes the form of charity work; other times, it takes the form of a business, such as Elon Musk's vision to transform transportation.

Truth Seeker

This personality comes in two flavors. Flavor 1 includes those who are devoted to their beliefs and want to spread the message or contribute to the success of their religion, group, or organization. Flavor 2 includes those who experience a lack of meaning or connection or have a problem—such as alcoholism or food addiction—and are seeking to fix their problem through a spiritual, psychological, scientific, or philosophical path, whether it be through formal religion, yoga, meditation, help groups (like AA or Codependent No More), or another ideology.

Although the second path may seem like an individual pursuit, I mention it because many people have taken it, leading them to connection and a desire to help others either by spreading information about their journey or by connecting with the community they are now a part of.

Your Philanthropic Mission

Your philanthropic mission is a part of your legacy and something you can pass on to your kids, grandchildren, and future generations. Part of it is explaining why you're passionate about giving; the other part is the action you take. You will lead by example.

To create an effective philanthropic mission, we must first understand the components that comprise a meaningful giving plan. Giving shouldn't feel like drudgery. If you're giving out of shame, obligation, or guilt, it's likely you haven't found what truly motivates you. If you're apathetic about giving or don't regularly give to others, it goes back to motivation issues—or it could just be that you're not in the habit or feel too overwhelmed with other things in life. Wherever you are is fine. You don't need to turn into Mother Teresa; there are times when giving is more feasible than other times.

The following is a practical approach to community involvement that meets you where you are and helps you expand to where you'd like to be.

Giving Component 1: Must Be Plausible for Your Lifestyle

How much free time do you have? How much time or money can you apply to an outside cause? Several studies have found that older adults who volunteer around one hundred hours per year (which works out to be approximately two hours per week) are happier and live longer than those who volunteer less of their time.[29] Volunteering more time than one hundred hours per year, however, does not improve these results. So, if possible, it's a good idea to spend approximately two hours per week giving to others and see how it affects you specifically.

The following are some guidelines to help you determine how you can spend your time and resources, depending on your situation:

If you have limited time and limited financial resources, think about one small thing you can do per month to help someone out or further a cause. You could visit your neighbors once a month with a plate of cookies. You could visit a retirement home and read to people there. Or you could volunteer at the local animal shelter.

If you have limited time and abundant financial resources, think about spending one or two hours a month planning how to "invest" your money in a cause you care about.

If you have ample time and abundant financial resources, try scheduling at least two hours a week to be involved with something you care about and plan how to spend your money in a way that is most beneficial to the cause.

---

29 Terry Y. Lum and Elizabeth Lightfoot, "The Effects of Volunteering on the Physical and Mental Health of Older People," *Research on Aging* 27 (2005): 31–55.

If you have ample time and limited financial resources, try spending at least two hours a week devoting your time to something you care about.

Giving Component 2: Must Tap into Your Values and Passions

What is your reason for giving? Is it to teach your children the importance of charity? Is it because someone at your church or work asked you to? Does it pump up your ego? Giving is similar to making money—when your heart isn't in it, it becomes a job. You don't want a job—you want a calling.

In the previous chapters, we discussed your Personal Legacy Statement and your family values, mission, and mantra. Your philanthropic mission will align with these values. But let's get more specific and think through how to identify your giving personality and pinpoint a cause that goes straight to the core.

Ask yourself these questions:

1. What causes have I contributed to in the past? Why did I contribute?

2. What struggles have I or my loved ones gone through? How did others help or could have helped?

3. Are there injustices that I have suffered or seen others suffer that make me angry or sad? What are they?

4. What do I love to do? Is there a way I could use that skill to help others?

5. What kind of advantages did I have as a child (or now) that I wish others could have?

6. Are there ways to improve my local community?

7. Am I religious? Do I want my religious beliefs involved?

8. How do I want to involve others through philanthropy? (Do I want my family involved? My employees?)

Write out the answers to these questions; they will unveil what you care about. I had a sister who was born with a heart condition and there was an amazing children's hospital that cared for her when she was little. I have a love for that hospital and for families who go through the heartache of having a child in the ICU. Because of this, I gravitate toward giving to this group of people because I can better empathize with them.

Another example is Ashley Nelson, the SVP of Fossil Group. She loves yoga and volunteers to teach it to women at a local prison. I know of another group of executives who teach inner-city boys how to fish. This experience helps them relive the excitement of their own childhood while connecting with these kids on a deeper level. In yet another example, the former CEO of Johnny Rockets contributes a significant amount to the university he attended because he was the first person in his family to graduate from college and he sees it as a big part of his legacy.

Giving Component 3: Must Analytically and Financially Make Sense

If you want to help curb poverty in third-world countries, there are a lot of great ideas to try: giving micro-loans, building schools, giving women aid, teaching the community farming techniques, or giving medical care. But be careful here: Some ideas look fantastic on paper and in practice fall short. Other ideas look dumb or sound too simplistic but work incredibly well in practice. Before you give your time and money to something, do some research to determine the best solution to the problem. Talk to different organizations and volunteers, and continue to ask questions and evaluate the effectiveness of the programs you're involved with.

Another variable to consider is the financial viability of the organization. Many nonprofits aren't financially viable on their own, meaning they don't have sufficient profit centers other than their donors. Other causes are self-sustaining, such as Tom's Shoes. Buy a pair, and that money funds a pair to go to someone else. Just because something doesn't run like a business and fund itself doesn't mean it's not a good idea. A lot of arts programs, community projects, and relief efforts are the result of generous givers.

Understanding which variables matter most to you is key. Certainly, solving the problem matters. But how do you feel about how the money is distributed? Do large salaries for nonprofit directors bother you? What about large marketing budgets—do you approve of the way funds are spent? Go to a site like www.charitynavigator.org and check out its evaluation criteria, where it rates charities based on their operating efficiencies. Some of the variables evaluated include program expense percentage, administrative expense percentage, fundraising expense percentage, fundraising efficiency, program expenses growth, working capital ratio, and liabilities to asset ratio. Even if you aren't involved in a larger charity or you're setting up your own, become familiar with these measurement metrics. You'll use them to determine where your organization's strengths and weaknesses lie.

The next thing to consider is how your giving impacts your individual financial situation. Different structures have different asset protection and tax advantages. Talk with a competent attorney who specializes in such things to determine what best suits your needs. A few years ago, I heard a speaker—a billionaire—at an event remark that he gave as much as he could to charity because he'd rather it go to charity than to the government. You may or may not agree with his philosophy, but you ought to know how your charity efforts affect your personal financial situation and structure your giving to receive optimal tax benefits.

Giving Component 4: Must Give You the Reward You Desire

I know this sounds like the opposite of giving, but giving is more sustainable when you get a great feeling from doing it. Determine what gives you that feeling. Is it the look of gratitude in someone's eyes when you give her a bag full of groceries so she can feed her family for another week? Is it the feeling of satisfaction you get from passing on your knowledge to someone else? Is it volunteering and working side by side with like-minded people? Structure your giving to generate more of that feeling. This could mean that you'd like to volunteer after a disaster, or that you prefer to serve on a board of advisors and plan the tactical side or vision of a philanthropic endeavor. It could mean you'd rather work one-on-one with a child. Or you may not want to work with people at all. Maybe you're creative and use your skills to sew blankets for babies in the ICU at your local hospital or design ornaments for a Christmas tree that is auctioned off for charity.

Seeing your family grow from their involvement in charity work may also motivate you. If you want your children or grandchildren to learn how to serve, walk your family through the process of evaluating their own passions for giving and have them report back to you and each other what their charity work taught them. One of the most effective ways to do this is through documenting their stories and memories on a website devoted to your philanthropic efforts.

Another fantastic idea is a closing ceremony or party after a charity event in which people share their experiences. Make sure someone records and archives it; the more tangible you can make it, the better. You could make a book with top quotes from the event and pictures of the project, or create a video or a blog post. These tactics can trigger that good feeling and remind yourself, your family, and others of the incredible work you all did and the difference everyone made. The more everyone is recognized for their good works, the more it becomes a part of who they are.

Creating Your Own Philanthropic System

Start small and ramp up from there to see what kind of philanthropic efforts appeal to you before you fully commit.

How to Start Small

Become a volunteer: Research organizations that focus on the cause you care about and volunteer. You can commit to limited time up front and get involved in different projects with different people.

Contribute money to a cause: Admittedly, I don't like

this one very much—at least, not by itself. The objective is to connect with a cause you care about and become involved. If you have limited time and can only contribute money right now, however, that's better than nothing. And, certainly, paying some sort of tithing or portion of your money to help others is significant. I'd recommend pairing donations with action—even if it's just one or two hours per month.

Join a board: Many nonprofits reach out to community leaders to serve on their board of advisors. You can help direct change through an organization that already exists on a more visionary level as one of several advisors. The time commitment is typically minimal, and your influence doesn't create the same impact as if it were your own organization, but your opinion matters.

Become a co-creator: Social Venture Partners (www. socialventurepartners.org) is a global organization with branches in many cities in the US, Canada, and larger cities around the world. Its model is based on pooling the money of local donors and using it to fund social projects within the area. But it doesn't stop with the money; those who donate want to be involved in improving the community. SVP facilitates this by educating its donors in determining which causes are best to fund and focusing on a theme for the year. Each year, SVP and its donor members vet applications and select one or two new groups to fund and support with their time, volunteer services, and organizational resources (such as HR, marketing, management, and leadership development). You may also want to co-create a project with another organization or a group of like-minded friends. You could speak with the director of your local hospital and set up a program helping kids there. Or you could create a yearly project with your business colleagues to beautify the community by planting flowers.

Set up a "smaller" structure: Talk with your attorney or financial team about how to structure your giving in a small way. A donor-advised fund, for example, gives you many of the same benefits of having your own private foundation without the burden and expense. There are a variety of options. Don't think you have to go "all in" at first. Getting your feet wet and then progressing to a larger structure when it makes sense can be a viable strategy.

Your Action Plan

Decide how often you're going to evaluate your charity efforts: monthly, quarterly, or yearly. Determine your goals, set a deadline, and think in actionable steps. How can you measure your efforts, and how will you hold yourself or your family accountable?

If you're exploring different philanthropic directions to determine your preferences, your goal could be something like:

I'm going to volunteer at one new organization per month for a year and at the end of that year determine which one I want to spend my time on.

If it's a shorter-term project and you want to get your kids involved, your goal could be something like:

> *Each one of us is going to start with $200 and invest it in our own charity idea. We will report back in one month about how we spent the money, who we helped, and how it made us feel.*

If it's a bigger, longer-term project, break it down into attainable goals. For example, perhaps you want to build and fund an orphanage in Nepal. The first milestone could be to survey the land and select the best area to build; the next milestone could be to generate support and find an avenue to select staff and workers locally in Nepal. My guess is that if you have a larger project like this in mind, you already have the ability to manage it or have a team who can do such a thing. The key here is taking action and ensuring your idea isn't just written in a notebook and stored away.

Entitlement and Your Kids

Born in 1980, I'm right on the bleeding edge of being a millennial—in no man's land—somewhere between Gen X and millennial. All the narcissistic labeling of millennials, however, makes me want to retreat to an earlier time, even if it means admitting I'm old. Those now in their twenties and early thirties have been labeled the "Me Me Me Generation," characterized by wiser elders as being selfish and entitled. We get married later (if at all), have fewer kids, post a plethora of selfies, and do crazy things—like go backpacking around Europe for two years while working from a laptop—all in an attempt to satisfy our thirst for purpose or pleasure.

The data is sobering. According to the National Institutes of Health, the incidence of narcissistic personality disorder is nearly three times as high for individuals in their twenties as for those in their mid-sixties or older. And how about the fact that 58 percent of college students scored higher in narcissism in 2009 than those did in 1982? There's a bunch of other scary statistics, from more young adults living with their parents than ever before to 40 percent of millennials feeling they should be promoted in their jobs every two years, no matter their level of competency.

Whether I'm at a dinner party or a financial conference, this narcissistic trend inevitably comes up when I talk about passing on values and wisdom to the younger generation. Many shrug and say, "Young people are just too entitled." Of course, I also run into people who have children or grandchildren who are loving, considerate, and grateful. And I've met some amazingly generous millennials. What I've noticed is that the difference between entitled and not entitled kids seems to be mostly about training.

If you ask most people—even of the Me Me Me Generation—if they want to help others, they'll say, "Yes!" But often they don't know how to go about it. Like any behavior, a focus on self is a habit and one that many employ simply because they don't know any better or they believe it will make them happier. It's counterintuitive that giving away your time, resources, and money to serve someone else could create more joy in your life, but that's what happens.

In experiments conducted by Elizabeth Dunn and her colleagues,[30] participants who were given $5–$20 to spend were happier when they spent the money on others instead of on themselves. The study also found that people who spent a

---

30 Elizabeth W. Dunn, Lara B. Aknin, and Michael I. Norton, "Spending Money on Others Promotes Happiness," Science 319 (2008): 1687–1688.

larger proportion of their income on others or contributing to a charity were happier than those who spent it on themselves.

The Darker Side of "Supposed" Narcissism

I remember listening to an interview with shame researcher Brené Brown in which she said she cringes whenever someone labels someone else a narcissist. According to her, these so-called narcissistic tendencies—such as posting selfies online—are an attempt for connection. As humans, we want to be seen and acknowledged. We want to be valued. To label someone "narcissistic" or "entitled" downplays their feelings and treats them as a joke. It's not kind and it's not recognizing their position.

Whether you have millions of dollars or are financially struggling, as a culture, we are conditioned to want to give our children a better life than what we had. We want to protect them; we want them to be successful. But unfortunately, the happiness trend for younger generations is moving in the wrong direction: A 2012 study by the American College Counseling Association reported a 16 percent increase in mental health visits since 2000. Also, suicide is the second leading cause of death among people aged twenty-five to thirty-five and the third leading cause of death among people aged fifteen to twenty-four.[31]

Everyone must find their own path to purpose and fulfillment, but how do we facilitate that for our children when we are seemingly living in a culture of purposelessness? The real problem is not in purposelessness itself but in the avoidance of pain. For some reason, "happiness" has come to mean

---

31 http://www.emorycaresforyou.emory.edu/resources/suicidestatistics.html

avoiding unpleasantness. But there are different seasons in life—highs and lows, mistakes followed by consequences. If we believe our lives are supposed to operate without hardship, we are in for a tough road when hardship inevitably befalls us. In his book *The Road Less Traveled*, M. Scott Peck writes, "Life is difficult. This is a great truth, one of the greatest truths. It is a great truth because once we truly see this truth, we transcend it. Once we truly know that life is difficult—once we truly understand and accept it—then life is no longer difficult. Because once it is accepted, the fact that life is difficult no longer matters." Helping others through their hardships, opening our minds to how others live and cope, and learning that life comes with difficulty is something to immerse our kids in. Otherwise, they cannot cope with harsh realities they've been protected from.

How Giving Helps

When we give to others, it takes us out of our reality, helps us empathize, and creates more love and connection. Instead of seeking connection through "trying to be cool" and getting the approval of others, we get it through sincerely giving and caring about someone's welfare.

I've found the best model for teaching kids to give is for the parents to be giving themselves. Children emulate their parents; if providing support and love to others is a part of your makeup, it's likely your children will prioritize that in their lives as well.

Think about your giving objectives in relation to your children. The following are some angles to consider when involving your family in community work.

Personal Development

Through selecting a charitable cause, your children can express their unique passions, opinions, and talents, and be creative and recognized. Some kids love charity work from the beginning, others feel obligated or pressured by their parents, and still others do it for ulterior reasons—such as creating a well-rounded application for college.

As a parent, you can't force anyone to feel a certain way. Your kids may feel discomfort in performing charity work. They may not "get it" until they find that thing they are truly passionate about. Maybe all your projects for feeding the homeless don't make your daughter excited, and then she finds out about a community garden project and her motivations change. All of a sudden, she's waking up at 5:00 a.m. and going to the garden before school.

When you make giving back a way to explore your children's talents and passions, it inspires confidence and a love of helping others.

Responsibility Training

The good thing about charity work is that it can be scaled up or down, depending on the competence, interest, and time availability of its participants. Many entrepreneurs and business executives I speak with are "go-getter" types, and I've noticed a trend in which they will try to get their children involved in entrepreneurial endeavors or try to push them toward ambitiously climbing the corporate ladder. This approach doesn't work for everyone. Being an entrepreneur is tough; it takes a certain temperament and ability to handle risk and instability. Certainly, your kids should know how to earn a living, but they may not end up being an ambitious business mogul. They may choose the path of an artist, a tour guide, an academic, or a concert musician.

Charity work can help them contribute to something they care about and exercise discipline. It helps them learn many of the same skills they would learn working in a business—teamwork, leadership, planning, and hitting deadlines—without the intense stress of the business environment and money motivations. These skills open up more opportunity and broaden their thinking. Depending upon your financial wealth, this kind of training may also be essential for your heirs to learn how to work with advisors, help manage a family office, or run your philanthropic foundation one day. Philanthropy is a common strategy estate planning attorneys and financial advisors use to train heirs to manage money and resources.

Building the Legacy of Your Family Name

One family I know gives money to the local hospital and makes a big deal about the family name being imprinted on a plaque on the building. From the outside looking in, this may seem like more narcissism. But it's not—at least, not from my point of view. When I spoke with the father, he said, "I want my kids to know our family stands for something and that we are building up the infrastructure of our community. It's an important lesson for my children to learn—that their family played a part in making this hospital great. When they grow up, I want them to look for ways they can improve their community and carry on our family name."

Teamwork and Bonding

When you work together, you grow closer. A charitable project can bring the family together. There are a variety of activities you can do as a family—vacations, family outings, dinners—and they all have their place. But there's something special about charity work. By nature, it's not flashy or self-indulgent (like a night of miniature golf followed by ice cream). It strikes at the root. When you see family members contributing to meaningful work, your respect for them increases.

When my father and mother were first dating, he was considering asking her to marry him, but something nagged him: They'd had only had fun times together. How did she react in challenging times? How did they respond to each other under stress? So they decided to build a grandfather clock together. Through sanding, cutting, gluing, and nailing, that clock gave them the ability to see another side of each other. My father could see how industrious my mother is: She would take a part that wasn't working, turn it around, play with it, and come up with a solution. He also saw that when she got flustered, she liked to take a break. She didn't like confrontation. That was okay—neither did he. And my mother saw how exacting my father was. He'd measure out each piece, carefully placing pencil marks in the crucial areas. He liked to plan things out. She liked to "eyeball it." If his measurements didn't work out the way he expected, he'd get in a thought loop and try to figure out the flaw in his schematics. It drove her a little crazy, but if she walked away for a few minutes, it was okay. Through this project, they saw their strengths and their weaknesses—and they worked together.

Charity work done right is like my parents building that

clock. When you work together with someone, your bond strengthens.

10

Systems for Living
Life Skills and Models of Communication

"In matters of style, swim with the current; in matters of principle, stand like a rock."

—Thomas Jefferson, American statesman and one of the Founding Fathers of the United States

Your legacy becomes reality when you put systems in place to ensure its longevity. Expecting your children to learn how to manage money, competently run your business, or even host a family event is not practical unless someone takes the time to teach them. Some skills and family philosophies will be learned through observation, which is a double-edged sword—your children may mimic things you'd rather not pass on—but many skills need to be taught.

Creating systems to teach important skills as well as providing a model for your heirs to follow by which they can carry on the family legacy is crucial. Otherwise, every generation or two, your family is likely to lose valuable information and move toward disorder while attempting to adapt to the changes around them. Whether you're trying to keep a fortune in tact or simply hoping to pass on a mindset of gratitude and independence, leaving this to chance is a recipe for failure.

As technology and worldviews change, so will your family. The idea is not to create systems so rigid they don't allow for innovation. Your systems should give your loved ones a foundation upon which they can build, empowering them to amend the systems as necessary.

The Comfort of Structure

When your children have a predicable path—a set of guidelines to direct them through to adulthood—it gives them a sense of security, even if they move away from that structure as they identify their own preferences. At present, many options have opened up for people living in first-world countries. It's not a given that you'll be married. Your gender roles have to be decided upon. Going to college doesn't guarantee you a good job. There is a growing gap between lower and upper classes, which means the rich are getting richer and the poor are getting poorer. This divide causes fear and sets up the reality that just because you work hard doesn't mean you'll be able to support your family or own a home. Fake news is running rampant, spreading ignorance and negativity.

Still, there's a lot to be hopeful for. The rate of medical and technological development is astounding. The average person has many tools available to reach significant numbers of people with an idea or business innovation. We can work from anywhere, travel, and experience things like never before. It's an exciting time to be alive.

If you are fortunate enough to have figured out how to create an abundant, happy life, passing on this knowledge to your family is critical. Your kids need to know how to navigate the world and, in many cases, create their own reality.

Three Systems Categories for Your Legacy

1. Systems to Educate

2. Systems to Foster Family Functioning and Cooperation

3. Systems for Legacy Development

We'll review each system category and the structure by which to implement and archive these systems.

Systems to Educate

Think about what skills, protocols and systems are important for your loved ones to know.

Also, think about skills you could teach. Maybe you could teach your granddaughter to ride a horse or your grandson how to sing. It's not just the skill you're passing on; it's also the experience. Learning how to cook from your grandmother (and making her cherished recipes) offers depth that's hard to find in a class taught by a stranger. The cooking becomes a medium to talk, express wisdom, and connect.

The following are topics to consider:

> **Mentorship Protocol:** How do young family members learn about family traditions, a good work ethic, forming healthy relationships, or running a business or philanthropy? How do you support family members in achiev-

ing their dreams?

Educational Experiences: What planned experiences have you created to encourage family members to teach each other or learn together?

Special Skills and Talents: What are your family's unique skills and talents? How do you intend to recognize or archive them?

Money Management: What does your family need to know about money? Who will teach them?

Systems to Foster Family Functioning and Cooperation

On a daily, weekly, or monthly basis, what does your family need to do to keep its relationships running smoothly? Family researcher Bruce Feiler[32] suggests holding a twenty-minute family meeting once a week and creating daily checklists. It's amazing how effective it is to have your six-year-old check off "get dressed" every morning; what used to be a daily negotiation can turn into autopilot for your kids and make both of your lives easier.

In addition to family meetings and daily checklists, also consider working toward family goals or coming up with a yearly family theme. Several families I've interviewed have themed vacations or retreats that focus on working together or learning new skills.

---

32 Author of *The Secrets of Happy Families.*

For example, let's say everyone in your family has been working too hard in their careers and at school, and you all need a break. Your theme for the year could be "Adventure," and your family goal could be to earn enough money to go to Costa Rica in the fall. According to studies, many people get more joy from the anticipation of an event than from the actual event itself in a phenomenon known as rosy prospection. Use this to your advantage by stretching out the planning process.

Principles for Designing Family Systems

When you hold a family meeting or plan a project, the following principles will make the process much more enjoyable:

No system is perfect, but strive for incremental improvement. Don't sweat it if your family doesn't run like a Swiss watch. It takes time, resolve, and incremental change to create something great. Your approach can change over time.

Children should be empowered. Let kids make executive decisions. It's easier for you and it also leads to kids who are more responsible, innovative, and confident.

Parents aren't dictators. Give everyone in the family an equal voice (within limits). You still create the framework and have veto power if an idea goes completely off the rails, but this usually doesn't happen.

Be open to serendipity. Keep your systems in place until you find something better, but keep an open mind and don't be afraid to try new approaches.

Don't attach love to performance. If someone makes a mistake, don't let them escape the natural consequence of their actions, but show your love unconditionally.

Family Governance for Significant Financial Assets

If you have significant financial assets or businesses and investments that require family members' input, work with your advisors to determine the best decision-making processes.

Systems for Legacy Development

In Chapter 4, we discussed writing your Personal Legacy Statement. Here, we cover what steps to take to develop a strong legacy. We also review processes to assist you in transferring your family legacy from one generation to the next.

Your Own Progression

Decide which systems will help you better realize your legacy objectives. On reviewing your Personal Legacy Statement, think about your philanthropic vision and how you would like to impact your family; consider goals or projects to enhance your personal progression.

Passing on a Family Legacy

A parent is often the glue that holds a family together. One man told me that when his mother was diagnosed with cancer, she made him promise to keep holding big family parties with his aunts, uncles, and cousins. She knew that if he didn't do it, no one else in the family would and they wouldn't be close anymore. Another family I know has appointed two CEOs for their family office: one CEO is more traditional and handles the financial and business side of the operation while the other CEO heads family development, ensuring the family meets together regularly, working with family members to ensure their health and emotional needs are taken care of, and planning bonding experiences to strengthen family ties.

Think about your own family legacy. Who plans family traditions? Who holds the family together? It's crucial to mentor family members to take over these roles as older generations age. Otherwise, when Grandma dies, that family closeness might disappear.

With your own family, consider how your beliefs, traditions, and systems will be passed on and what system can ensure your family's longevity over generations. Much like an association with appointed leadership to manage its members, your family may benefit from appointing someone to plan the cultural activities for the family or create a family counsel who helps family members as changes occur. This family counsel, for example, could develop a process to introduce a new spouse into the family and make them feel welcome or come up with solutions when family disagreements arise.

The Family Brain Trust

Your family systems are not very useful unless you have them organized so each family member can access and share them. This system of keeping track of your valuable family insights, knowledge, and skills is called a Family Brain Trust.

Consider how information is passed from one person to another through oral traditions, writing, video/audio, and training or experience-based learning. Although it makes sense to discuss your insights, mere talk doesn't have a lasting effect. There's a reason the Bible is printed: The printed word has a permanency to it. Without the written word, it would be hard for Christianity to have survived for thousands of years.

Technology opens up all kinds of documentation processes that were not available in the past. Anyone can create a library of high-quality audio, video, or written information with little expense. Think about what formats appeal most to you and start documenting.

I recommend documenting your family information on a password-protected website as well as making it physically available (e.g., print books, pictures or documents and distribute them to family members or store them in a safe deposit box). A website is convenient, allowing for instant access and contribution, but it likely won't survive in its exact form for generations, so use it as a tool to extract information and archive it in the short term, but also plan for long-term documentation.

Principles of Effective Brain Trusts

When you create your Family Brain Trust website and file storage system, keep these principles in mind:

> **Accessible from Multiple Locations**: Your Brain Trust houses information that can help your loved ones, but it can't help them if they can't get to it easily. This library of resources must be available to any member of your family at any time, which is why a website is such a good idea.

We have a system for our clients that is specifically set up for creating an online family legacy, but there are a variety of alternatives if you want to format a website on your own.

Encourages Contribution: Every member of the family should be allowed to contribute. One voice shouldn't drown out the others. Certainly, older generations may have been through more, but younger generations can also add a ton of value. Consider assigning family research projects or learning about something together and having everyone contribute their ideas. For example, have everyone research how to be healthy, and each member of the family could contribute their favorite books, tips, and routines to that end.

Easy to Archive: Again, you don't want your family information stuck in a website that becomes obsolete over time. Think of all the family memories that are on old 8mm films or slides—these now need to be converted over to a usable format. Digital information is scarier, however, because there's no physical representation of it; at least with an 8mm film, you've got a reel of it somewhere. When digital formats become obsolete, there's no physical trace except for a failing hard drive. Periodically, you'll want to download your information, store it in a safe place digitally (on a hard drive or thumb drive), and print it.

Structured to Make Information Sharing Easy: It's hard to share your knowledge when there's no structure. If an interviewer began with, "Tell me everything you know," you'd have a hard time reeling off your wisdom. It's too broad. So don't do the same thing with your Brain Trust. You need a website with sections and categories so your loved ones understand what you expect from them. A website with a variety of pre-set categories (as well as the option to add your own) allows for more intelligent responses and helps your family generate ideas.

Some categories we use with our websites are:

1. Gratitude Board: This is where your family posts what they love about other members of the family and to express appreciation.

2. Favorites: Where family members list their favorite recipes, memories and traditions.

3. About Us: Family mission, mantra, coat of arms and other identity elements.

4. Legacy Letters: Letters from each family member to their loved ones to be passed on as a part of their estate plan.

5. Words of Wisdom: Money advice, business advice, health advice, exercises like having your family answer the question "What is the most important thing I learned this year?"

*Visit **www.meaninglegacytools.com** for a full listing of the categories we use and to learn more about how to create your own online Family Brain Trust.*

11

Public Presence
Who You Are Online

"A good reputation is more valuable than money."
—Publilius Syrus, Latin writer and philosopher

Some people are concerned about their public reputation, while others couldn't care less. In my opinion, however, your public presence should be closely managed. Privacy isn't as valued now as it used to be, and there's a lot of information online about everyone. Even if you aren't particularly famous, it's likely you have a digital footprint. This creates some interesting conundrums for those who value privacy or who ardently avoid creating a digital presence.

The first conundrum is that people expect you to have an online presence and they will typically do a mini-background check; whatever comes up online will be their impression of you. The second is that others will post information about you, including media outlets, companies, friends, family, employees, and colleagues, and you don't want to leave your reputation up to their random opinions of you.

Who you are online becomes your legend. This is what future (and current) generations will know you as. Some additional benefits of a well-thought-out public legacy include:

- The establishment of a reputation that leads to more business deals, greater networking, or philanthropic opportunities.

- The ability to more widely spread a message of what you care about and effect change.

- Greater approachability.

- Higher resiliency in the face of attack or a public relations (PR) disaster.

- The creation of a well-respected family name and legacy for your children to be proud of.

- The ability to keep in touch with friends, colleagues, and acquaintances.

I won't delve too heavily into the dark side of one's public legacy here; suffice it to say that we are all highly vulnerable. In his book *Trust Me, I'm Lying*, Ryan Holiday describes the ease with which someone—anyone who has average skills as a manipulator—can get blog writers and eventually big media to publish a lie. Entire careers have been destroyed by one nasty gossiper. And, unfortunately, although I'd like to tell you your reputation is under your control, it's not. These lies can turn into a Pandora's box of disaster.

What is under your control is what you release to the public and how you cultivate your public persona. How you position yourself, react, and maneuver can make a huge difference in how you are ultimately perceived.

Assessing Your Current Status

The first step in determining your online effectiveness is to conduct an audit. Google yourself, and see what pops up. It could be your LinkedIn profile, an unsecured Facebook page listing your family photos, news articles about your company, and so on. Surf the first couple of pages. Try a few different key terms, like your last name mixed with your city, your company name, and your spouse's name. What kind of impression would a stranger get if they only learned about you online?

Now search for people you admire and those you despise. You can do some searches of people who have already passed on, but try to keep this in the realm of the living. You want to see what others are doing and get ideas for yourself. Conduct an analysis of each person's online profile and write down what you admire as well as where you believe they have failed.

Search for Richard Branson, Donald Trump, Warren Buffett, Steve Martin, Taylor Swift, and Mark Cuban. Now search for those you most respect in your field of business. Search for your competitors. Search for your favorite musicians and actors. Search for your favorite authors. Search for the guy who bullied you in high school. Then try your neighbors, your best friend, or your children.

How does each profile differ? What aligns with your personal brand? What doesn't? What have they done well? After looking at these profiles, what would you like to incorporate as a part of your public presence?

Notice if certain industries have a particular way of presenting themselves. What is credible in the banking industry is completely boring for the celebrities of the TV show *Real*

Housewives. Notice who appears credible, who appears narcissistic, and who appears ridiculous. What are commenters saying about them? What kinds of photos, videos, and posts seem to work well and get the most attention? Do they talk about their families or personal lives?

What about generation gaps? If you look at the profile of a teen musician compared to that of someone who has been in the industry for several decades, what kinds of differences do you see? Do they use different language? Is it important to you to appeal to younger generations and appear relevant?

Read the *New York Times* or *Wall Street Journal* and find a few people who are going through a PR disaster. Look them up. How are they responding to the attack? What strategies are effective? What is leading to more blow ups? (You may want to look at past PR disasters and track the progress or follow a current one for a few months to see what happens.)

Next, search for companies and nonprofits you care about, such as the American Red Cross, Tom's Shoes, or local charities. Search for the top businesses in your industry, as well as large and small companies you admire. How do these companies represent themselves? Do the key executives emphasize their own stories, or is it all about the company?

This exercise is all about getting familiar with what others are doing so that you can best map out your own presence.

How to Create Your Digital Legacy

Here's your blueprint for creating a strong digital legacy:

1. Decide what kind of presence you want to have and the scope of that presence.

   a. Professional—for your business or career.

   b. Personal—to connect with family and friends.

   c. Community focused—to improve the world or support a charity or cause you care about.

   d. Passion focused—to spread your love of cooking, art, writing, golf, or whatever you're into.

2. Understand you are building the online "legend" of yourself. You are creating a narrative about who you are, and you must consider how that story is going to evolve. Ask yourself: What do I care about? How do I want to connect with others? What do I want to share?

3. Develop a public mission statement and vision and make sure your posts, communications, and pictures support that vision. You want to represent a cohesive message online and establish yourself as someone who represents a strong vision.

4. Monitor your presence and manage what is being said about you. Put your name on Google Alerts and be aware of how you are being represented online by others.

5. Always tell the truth. If you're trying to cover up a scandal or create a public persona that doesn't exist in real life, it'll come back to bite you—hard.

6. Understand that the more public you are, the more likely you are to make a blunder. Don't get overly paranoid here, but don't ever be flippant with your social media posts (unless you're one of the creators of South Park or something similar that is in alignment to your brand). A misinterpreted joke or photo can lead to all kinds of hell.

Bill Gates Redefined

Bill Gates is now one of the most admired men in the world, but it wasn't always that way. Remember when the government was after him for running a monopoly? His cadre of lawyers fought hard and reached a favorable settlement, but it left the public with a bad aftertaste—and that's when he started really focusing on philanthropy.

Bill and Melinda Gates have done a tremendous amount of good in this world, but they also were extremely strategic in how they positioned the Bill & Melinda Gates Foundation in the media. It didn't take long for "Gates, the greedy software opportunist" to turn into "Gates, the man who's devoted to reforming healthcare and education for a better world." What made this strategy viable is that, as far as anyone can tell, Bill and Melinda Gates are sincere in their efforts and they aren't covering up lies or character deficits. In other words, if philanthropy is only used to enhance reputation or cover up heinous acts, it will backfire. But it doesn't hurt to use your status and influence for a mission for good and publicize it. The number of lives their foundation has impacted and the number of influential people they have involved in their vision is astounding, ranking Bill and Melinda Gates as the second most generous philanthropists in America; Warren Buffet, who shares control of the foundation with Bill and Melinda, is ranked number one.

Martin Luther King Jr., Eleanor Roosevelt, John F. Kennedy, and Andrew Carnegie all went down in history as greats because they had something in common: a greater vision for the future that was made public. Their contribution went beyond wealth or accomplishment; it was well chronicled and appealed to the public in the right way at the right time. Do you want to go down in history as being one of the greats? Then your accomplishments must be documented and promoted in the right way, or you risk falling into obscurity.

There are two kinds of leaders: one who pursues goals for the sake of becoming famous—for the recognition of it—and the other who pursues goals for the sake of accomplishing something great. The first is dangerous. The second changes the world for the better. A strong leader of a noble cause is something the public will always gravitate toward. We want to follow great men and women. We want examples of excellence. We want to feel hopeful and inspired. If you have something—a humanitarian effort, a business idea, or an invention—that you believe will make a great impact and improve people's lives, it is your responsibility to spread it. If you'd rather keep your head down and avoid the personal attention of publicity, that's your prerogative. But consider ways to attract attention to your cause, even if you are not the face of it.

12

Sharing It All

Leaving Love Letters

"If you would not be forgotten as soon as you are dead, either write something worth reading or do something worth writing."

—Benjamin Franklin, American author, publisher, scientist, inventor, and one of the Founding Fathers of the United States

In his book *The Like Switch*, former FBI communication and body language specialist Jack Schafer writes about how to avoid divorce. His advice is to write love letters to each other when you are madly in love and put them in a box. And then, when the love inevitably fades and you are questioning your marriage, you should go to the box, take out the letters, and read them to remind yourself why you fell in love in the first place.

The creation of books, videos, audio content, letters, photo albums, and works of art that capture your legacy is like that box of love letters. You don't know when someone you love is going to need your support. It could be tomorrow or fifty years from now. Your story could be a lifeline to help them better understand themselves, feel greater love, or see their lives with greater perspective.

I know a woman who found her grandfather's handwritten journal from when he was a young man and serving in the army in the second World War. At the time, she was about the same age as he was when he had written in it. Although she'd never met him, his journal made a major impact on her life. She was struggling to decide which career to pursue, and there was something about what he said in his journal that helped her confidently proceed on the best path forward.

In the coming pages, we will cover how to approach passing on your non-financial assets and ways you can craft your legacy for ultimate receptiveness.

The Aesthetic Experience

"The aim of art is to represent not the outward appearance of things, but their inward significance."
—Aristotle

According to psychologists Gerald C. Cupchik and Andrew S. Winston (1996),[33] aesthetic experience is a psychological process in which attention is focused on the object while all other objects, events, and everyday concerns are suppressed. In other words, focusing on artwork, a play, or natural scenery, or even the process of creating can allow us to transcend everyday life and have an almost magical experience. There can be a similar effect when we listen to music, participate in

---

33 G. C. Cupchik and A. C. Winston, "Confluence and Divergence in Empirical Aesthetics Philosophy and Mainstream Psychology," *Handbook of Perception & Cognition: Cognitive Ecology* (San Diego, CA: Academic Press, 1996).

dance, or read creative writing (such as poetry or engaging stories).

Your objective in sharing your legacy with others is not just to transfer knowledge—it's also to connect emotionally. When you speak to someone's emotional side, their experience is heightened. You want to take your loved ones (and yourself, for that matter) through a creative journey of discovery, surprise, and personal reflection.

Consider these examples of aesthetic engagement vs. the mundane:

Example 1: Family Tree

Mundane: You read a list of names to your granddaughter and tell her they are all a part of her family tree.

Aesthetic: You show your granddaughter an illustration of your family tree with drawings of each of your ancestors and small scenes depicting their life's journey. You point out the details and tell her there is a violin for her great-grandmother because she played in a symphony orchestra, and a boat for her grandfather because he sailed around the world. Suddenly, she's engaged and wants to hear more about the stories of each ancestor.

Example 2: Legacy Letter

Mundane: You tell your son you love him and that he's grown into a wonderful young man.

Aesthetic: On your son's twenty-first birthday, you give him a letter describing what you admire about him and how proud you are. In it, you tell the story about how you learned about the importance of integrity (when your mother dragged you to the store as a five-year-old and you had to apologize for stealing a piece of candy) and what you hope for your son in the future.

Example 3: Family Health Musical

Mundane: You decide that, as a family, you would like to start making healthier choices. So you assign each member of the family a topic to research and report back on.

Aesthetic: After deciding as a family that you'd like to start making healthier choices, you assign each family member a topic to research and report back on. But here's the catch: They have to report the information in less than five minutes and do it in the form of a poem or a song.

Example 4: Holiday Celebration

Mundane: On Thanksgiving, you go around the table and say what you're thankful for.

Aesthetic: On Thanksgiving, you hang large poster paper on the wall and have everyone in the family write what he or she is thankful for and draw a picture to go along with it. Afterward, you take a photo of it and send it to everyone.

Creating an aesthetic experience takes time and thought, but it's worthwhile because it converts a run-of-the-mill activity into one you can treasure.

Legacy Vehicles

Just as there are financial vehicles—trusts, foundations, and wills—that help pass on financial assets, there are legacy vehicles to help pass on non-financial assets. Below is a list of some legacy vehicles to consider including as a part of your estate plan.

Website: You can blog about your family experiences or post on social media. My recommendation is to have a password-protected site that only family members can access. I have some website platform recommendations at www.meaninglegacytools.com. A family website should have an area where you can post your coat of arms, your principles, stories and memories, photos and videos, favorite recipes, traditions, events, legacy letters, and more.

Wisdom Memoir™: A Wisdom Memoir is different from the generalized story of your life. It's purposeful and written with the intent of passing on wisdom. No matter how much your family loves you, they are not going to want to sift through pages of random thoughts about growing up. A Wisdom Memoir has a clear topic, includes a story arc, and is meant to engage your reader. For example, you could write a memoir specifically about food and its preparation in your home. You could start with your grandmother and memories you have of cooking with her, then talk about your mother, and finally your experience cooking for your family and involving your children. A Wisdom Memoir can be long (hundreds of pages) or short (a quick essay or a 200-word blog post).

Specialty Books: Like Wisdom Memoirs, specialty books have a specific purpose or topic. You could create a book for your daughter when she gets married, compile memories from different family members into a book about traditions, or create an illustrated children's book that explains where your granddaughter came from.

Legacy Letters/Ethical Wills: A legacy letter is a concise document that expresses your love for either your entire family or for a specific person. The original idea was for a parent or loved one to write down words of wisdom, advice, and love to be passed on to their heirs when they died. But I'm finding that writing a legacy letter for your son, for example, and sharing it with him while you're still alive allows you to communicate and express love on a deeper level. You don't want to wait until the end of your life to tell your family how much you love them. Writing a legacy letter and sharing it can be the conduit for expressing what may have been difficult before, and it's completely doable. You don't have to write some big book or catalog your whole life. Write a page or two about your feelings and share the letter. It will be something your family treasures now and in the future.

Videos/Audio Content: Creating video or audio content is the next level of capturing someone's essence. It adds so much more depth when you can hear their voice and see their mannerisms. Like Wisdom Memoirs, videos and audios should be purposeful and focus on a specific topic.

Paintings, Wall Hangings, Photos, Art: Would you like to have an illustration of your family tree hanging on your wall? What about photos of your children or wall hangings featuring your family rules or mantra? Consider visual representations of your legacy that will remind you about what you represent.

Family Coat of Arms, Mission, Mantra, Rules: Document your family brand on your website, in a book, or as art pieces that hang around your home. The more visual, the better. Decide what formats are best for you and your family.

Keepsakes: There's that vase you got on your honeymoon in Italy. And the teapot your grandmother gave you. Consider putting together a document or even video or audio content that tells the story of your most cherished possessions. Speak with your children (or inheritors) about these keepsakes and share their stories. This could lead to discussions about who gets what when you die. If you're not ready to talk about it, tell them you're still deciding and that this time is about explaining the history of each item.

If you are ready to have the who-gets-what conversation, it's often better to decide now than to leave your kids to fight about it after you're gone. If you have highly valuable keepsakes, talk with an attorney about their transfer before you bring it up with your heirs. A competent attorney can help you work through potential issues.

Family Brain Trust: Make sure you have a place—a website or a file—to store family information; encourage your family members to participate.

Yearly Meaning Snapshot™: A legacy is not fixed—it's always evolving as people grow. The Yearly Meaning Snapshot is something we do at our company, and you can create something similar with your own family. It's a two-page spread about each member of your family, their accomplishments, and most important stories, lessons, and joys over the last twelve months. It also includes notable photos or visual representations of that person. The idea is that, over time, you will have two pages that represent each family member's life for each year. These pages can be compiled into a book for that person, or all the profiles for the family can be included in the same book. You can also have the content in a digital format and create audio content or videos with interviews of each family member.

Public Legacy Campaign: If you have a message or philanthropic cause you'd like to promote in your community or the world, there's a variety of collateral pieces to consider. Websites, videos, brochures, social media accounts, PR and advertising campaigns, and more.

Creation Process

The creation of each legacy vehicle will need to be planned and carefully executed. I spent over a decade running a creative firm that designed websites, videos, books, and magazines for companies, and my company now works with families in creating similar content. So a lot of this is second nature to me. I can see the project in my head, plan it out, bring in the right players, and direct the creation of the content. Many people, however, do not have this background. And it's best to consider your strengths.

If you are creative and love projects, research examples of what you'd like to accomplish and begin modeling the pieces that speak to you. If you don't consider yourself to be creative, find others to help with the project, whether it's a whole team of experts, family members, or friends. It all depends on your vision, who you trust to help, and your budget.

Although the creation of each legacy vehicle is an art in itself and could easily take a whole book to explain, I'm going to give you some general guidelines.

Raw Content vs. Crafted Content

There's a big difference between having stacks of journals—detailing everything from what you ate for breakfast to how nervous you were to raise your hand in class to why you left your boyfriend—and having a well-written book about a specific topic. Will your kids really want to sift through the journals? It may be interesting for the first few pages, but it gets old pretty fast. To communicate the most important parts of yourself, you must craft them in a way that is engaging, is respectful of the reader's time, and has a point.

No matter what you create, ask yourself, "What is the purpose of this piece?" Consider your audience. What will connect with them? They will remember the average of what you said. In other words, it's better to focus on the top five most important points than to try to squeeze in fifty-five, where, after a while, none of it will seem that significant. Think about how you want to be remembered and keep the message simple.

Creating with Intent

Before you begin writing, filming, or painting, think about why you're creating this legacy vehicle. It's much easier to work with purposeful raw content than raw content that's all over the place. If you don't define your intention for the content up front, you could end up with twenty hours of video interviews with your grandmother, only to realize at the end of it that you didn't ask the most important questions for your project. It's much better to "guide the actor" from the beginning. In my course about interviewing your family for their stories, I recommend filling out a story arc worksheet in the pre-interview. (Get a complimentary copy of the worksheet for your own use at www.meaninglegacytools.com.) On it, you list your interviewee's key story points so they know the structure of an engaging story before the camera starts rolling. It is very focused, considers the enjoyment of the audience, and gives the presenter more structure, therefore making them feel more confident.

Modeling the Best

There's no need to reinvent the wheel. Spend some time searching for the best examples of what you'd like to create. Do you want to film a video about your mother's life? Great. Now search for documentaries or video biographies about great women. How did they film the interview? What worked well, and what was boring or awkward?

You can apply the same process to the creation of any content piece—memoirs, biographies, audio content, or websites. Ask yourself what went into creating the content to reverse-engineer the piece.

Distributing and Archiving

To Whom It Should Go (and When)

Make a list of each of your legacy vehicles and determine who you'd like to pass them on to. A certain legacy vehicle may be for only one person, your whole family, or your friends. Consider the following questions when filling out your list of legacy vehicles and determining who inherits them:

1. **Who benefits most? To whom are you obligated?** If you've ever put together an invite list for a wedding, you know there are those you want to be there and those you're obligated to invite (such as your mom's crazy best friend). Passing on legacy vehicles is similar. Maybe you know your memoir will be well received by your youngest daughter, but leaving your other two children out of it because you fear their criticism will cause a rift in the family. Decide how you'd like to handle this before it happens. Legacy vehicles are meant to bring family together, not tear it apart.

2. **When is the best time?** There is a temptation to delay writing a legacy letter or putting your memoir together until "later." At some later time, you reason, you'll be less busy. But the sad reality is we never know when we won't be around. On a less morbid note, you'd be absolutely amazed by how close your family can become when you start thinking through your legacy and putting together legacy vehicles. When you make your legacy a priority, your lens changes and everything becomes more mean-

ingful. It's for this reason that I believe it's an extremely good idea to pass on legacy vehicles as soon as possible. A celebration of your anniversary accompanied by a book you distribute to your whole family about how much you love them and the lessons you've learned can be so special, and the book becomes a treasured possession that can be passed on.

3. **Who would it benefit right now?** Not everyone is going to benefit from your legacy vehicles equally in the same time frame. For example, let's say you wrote a book about how to be happily married. Should you give that to your 10-year-old grandson? Probably not. It's best to wait until he gets engaged or, at least, until he starts dating. There also may be some advice or training that benefits one child greatly right now but holds little value for the others. For example, if you are experienced in real estate and your daughter is interested in buying and flipping her first house, you may spend extra time educating her about the process. Sure, general principles about real estate investment may be a part of your Family Brain Trust, but your daughter's interest in it could take it to a whole new level that benefits not only her but also others in the future (if you document it right) when they are ready to do something similar.

4. **What does waiting accomplish?** According to a recent survey,[34] nearly 30 percent of family leaders have no plans to share inheritance details out of fear of demoti-

---

34 In 2017, Campden Wealth, the Institute for Private Investors, and Wilmington Trust conducted a survey of fifty-seven research participants who belong to families with a net worth of at least $20 million—72 percent of which had a net worth of over $50 million—entitled "Navigating the Wealth Transfer Landscape."

vating heirs. What fears do you have about sharing your legacy vehicles? Determine if they are founded or not. Sharing your legacy vehicles usually leads to building trust and creating closeness. But it may not always be the best idea for your particular situation.

5. **What legal implications will it have?** Sharing family stories, making traditions, and defining your family mission statement isn't likely to have any legal ramifications. But talking about the significance of financial assets or starting conversations about who should run the business or get money from the family bank could lead to legal issues. If you are concerned, consult your attorney or financial advisors before starting conversations that may cause your heirs to make assumptions that you cannot legally or financially back up.

6. **How often does this legacy vehicle need updating?** Some legacy vehicles are one-time projects and don't ever need to be updated—such as a book you write about memories of your parents. Other legacy vehicles should be updated regularly—such as your Family Brain Trust or legacy letters. Determine how often you'd like to update each legacy vehicle and review your legacy plan in general. A yearly check-in is a good idea.

Privacy

We live in a world where privacy is eroding. Make sure your family knows what details to keep private. What may seem obvious to you—like not sharing family stories on Facebook—could be something they've never even considered.

Healthy Storage Environment

For physical items—books, keepsakes, film reels, photos, a physical coat of arms—consider what conditions will ensure the items are preserved but also enjoyed. If your family cannot flip through a book because they worry about ruining it, the purpose of it is defeated. Convert electronic files or information on social media or website platforms to a physical format (i.e., print them); also, save them in a few places so the data isn't lost, like on an external hard drive, in the cloud, or on a website.

Also, be aware of changing formats. Flash, for example, used to be huge for developing animated presentations, interactive websites, and videos. Now, because Apple decided not to support it on its devices several years ago, Flash has faded. You'll also see this phenomenon with certain apps—where you can only open the file within the app and nowhere else. Be sure your audio, video, image, and document files are in a popular format and can be easily accessed by standard programs. If formats change over time, convert your files before they become unusable.

Legacy Vehicle Transfer

Decide how to transfer electronic files to the right people at the right time. You could leave instructions to your attorney or trust executor, give your family a login to your family website, leave an external hard drive in your safe deposit box, or share a folder on Dropbox. Distinguish between what is "public" and what is only for their eyes. Logins to your accounts, bank data, and medical information should be cataloged somewhere in case you are incapacitated and your family needs to access it. Understand the difference in levels of security. Your bank account information, for example, should be encrypted and protected behind complicated passwords. Your memoir, on the other hand, may just be a file with no protection at all.

Physical items are more difficult to transfer because, by their nature, they are limited. Decide who will receive physical items and when. If it's sentimental with little monetary value—such as a family book, legacy letter, coat of arms, or family photos—you can decide who they should go to and transfer whenever it makes sense. For many items, it's possible to have multiple copies made due to on-demand printing and the ease of which we can now make scanned copies, duplicates of photos, or multiple books. If you have several copies of the same content, distribute them to the appropriate family members and save a copy as a part of your physical archives. If your physical items have monetary value—such as your grandfather's stamp collection or a classic car—speak with an estate planning attorney before you begin transferring these items.

Consider the significance of passing on physical items. Try to make it special and meaningful—at a wedding, just before graduation during a meaningful one-on-one conversation, or at a ceremony during a family reunion. If you treat these items with reverence, your family will too.

PART 3

CASE STUDIES

The following case studies will give you an idea about how we approach constructing a Meaning Legacy Plan at Paragon Road. They are for illustrative purposes only and do not describe specific clients.

13

Newlyweds
Case Study

Situation

Julie and John are in their late twenties. They are planning to be married in eight months and have reserved a beautiful spot overlooking the beach for the big day. Julie picked out lavender and spring green as her colors, and she and John are not sure if they like the poppy seed cake or strawberries and cream, but they have a while to decide.

"We want our lives to start off right," Julie says.

"Exactly," John replies and pats Julie's hand. "That's why we're planning our family legacy now. We've seen what happens to people who don't have a plan. Life can toss them all over and they end up miserable or divorced. That's not happening to us. We want to create something special."

"Also," Julie smiles, "I know it's a little silly, but I want a spectacular coat of arms to display at our wedding party! It's so meaningful to have those added touches."

Objectives

In an initial Meaning Legacy planning meeting, Julie and John outline the following objectives:

1. To create solid principles and rules by which we live our lives.

2. To build one of the best marriages possible. We want to grow more deeply in love each year.

3. To create a family brand that represents excellence.

4. To accomplish our joint dreams and goals for the future.

5. To create a stable, loving home for our future children.

Strategy

Our team spends a day with John and Julie outlining their vision and gathering crucial information to construct their Meaning Legacy Plan. From there, we plan several meeting times to explain each step of the process and develop their creative content. After the initial meetings and creative content is complete, we set up a schedule for continued yearly legacy check-ins.

Outcome

Comprehensive Family Meaning Legacy Plan. The purpose of this plan is to outline the goals, values, principles, and ways John and Julie would like to raise their children and envision their legacy. It also provides specific instructions for implementation and lists immediate and long-term milestones.

Coat of Arms. Our creative team works with John and Julie to conceptualize a coat of arms that represents the legacy they want to leave behind.

Rituals and Traditions. We work with John and Julie to plan specific traditions that will support their objectives of falling more deeply in love and creating a stable, loving home. These include "I love you" romance rituals, weekly family meetings, yearly family growth retreats, holiday traditions, and a Yearly Meaning Snapshot.

The Story of Us Book™. This is the visual representation of John and Julie's family Meaning Legacy Plan. It has a beautiful printout of their coat of arms, their principles, master stories (i.e., stories about their childhood memories, how they first met, their parents), heritage and family tree, and their Personal Legacy Statements.

Stories of Love Anthology™. This is a book of short stories from friends, loved ones, and relatives about John and Julie and their family. It is a way to commemorate their wedding day and a keepsake they can show to future generations.

Yearly Meaning Snapshot. We create a two-page spread for each member of John and Julie's family—one for John, Julie, and each of their parents—that outlines their accomplishments, and their most important stories, lessons, and joys over the last twelve months. It also includes notable photos or visual representations of that person. As they have children, they will create one for their family members and each child every year in June, around the time of their anniversary. Over time, they will have two pages that represent each family member's life for that year. These pages can be complied into a book for that person, or all the profiles for the family can be included in the same book. We also provide a digital format and audio or video formats with interviews of each family member. The pages are printed on archival paper that can either be framed, stored in a safe place, or included in a book.

File Storing and Sharing. We create a place for John and Julie to store their most important files and set up a family website that the family can use to share stories, ideas, and memories.

Newlyweds

Case Study

Objectives

1. To create solid principles and rules by which we live our lives.

2. To build one of the best marriages possible. We want to grow more deeply in love each year.

3. To create a family brand that represents excellence.

4. To accomplish our joint dreams and goals for the future.

5. To create a stable, loving home for our future children.

Meaning Legacy™ Plan

Detailing goals, values, principles, and ways John and Julie would like to raise their children and implement their legacy.

Coat of Arms

Representative of the family's principles. Printed on archival paper, then framed and displayed at their home.

Rituals & Traditions

A plan of weekly, monthly and yearly traditions, including a family growth retreat and "I love you" romance rituals.

Stories of Us Book™

Includes the coat of arms, their principles, master stories, heritage and family tree, and their Legacy Statements.

Results

Stories of Love Anthology™

Book of short stories from friends, loved ones, and relatives about John and Julie and their family.

Yearly Meaning Snapshot™

Two-page spread for each member of John and Julie's family that outlines their accomplishments, and their most important stories, lessons and joys over the last year.

File Storing and Sharing

A place for John and Julie to store their most important files and a website where the family can share stories, ideas, and memories.

14

Parents with Young Kids
Case Study

Situation

Allison and Jason have been married for ten years. He is the CEO of a large technical company in the Bay Area. She was a corporate attorney but left her firm when they had their first child to focus on parenting. She also spends a portion of her week working with a nonprofit she is passionate about. Allison and Jason now have three children: a nine-year-old daughter, a seven-year-old son, and a three-year-old son.

"Our family is the most important thing to us," Allison says.

"Yep," Jason agrees. "But, admittedly, I'm a little terrified for my daughter to become a teenager. How do we keep her on a good path? Right now, she looks up to me, but I know that's going to change. We try our best to talk about what it means to be a good person and teach our children what matters, but nothing is very systematic."

"What legacy means to us," Allison interjects, "is creating

a strong family and giving our children the skills they need to be happy in life, and serve others."

"But it can be hard," Jason says. "We are both busy. The kids are a handful. Sometimes daily life gets in the way and we don't act like model parents, or our house is mayhem with screaming kids and chaos—just getting them to bed can be a major victory."

Objectives

In an initial Meaning Legacy planning meeting, Allison and Jason outline the following objectives:

1. To create solid principles and guidelines to increase love, loyalty, and peace within our home.

2. To make time for our relationship and personal growth.

3. To create a family brand that represents love.

4. To create systems within the home to decrease the amount of chaos and increase our children's responsibility.

5. To prepare our children to become independent people who have high self-esteem, gratitude, a sense of responsibility, passion, and competence, and who are ready to leave the nest when they are old enough.

Strategy

Our team spends a day with Allison and Jason gathering crucial information to construct their Meaning Legacy Plan. From there, we plan several meeting times to go through each step of the process and develop their creative content. After the initial meetings and creative content is complete, we set up a schedule for continued yearly legacy check-ins.

Outcome

Comprehensive Family Meaning Legacy Plan. The purpose of this plan is to outline the goals, values, principles, and ways they'd like to raise their children, and the vision for Allison and Jason's legacy. It also provides specific instructions for implementation and lists immediate and long-term milestones.

The First Family Meeting. We meet with the whole family and begin to construct the family mission, mantra, family rules, and values with the children. The nine-year-old is precocious and has a lot of ideas, the seven-year-old keeps to himself, and the three-year-old gets excited whenever someone asks him about his toy truck. Most of the ideas come from Allison and Jason, but little touches from the kids add to the process and make it something the whole family can get excited about.

Coat of Arms. Our creative team works with Allison and Jason to conceptualize a coat of arms or family logo that represents the legacy they want to leave behind.

Rituals and Traditions. We work with Allison and Jason to plan specific traditions that will support their objectives of creating the kind of family and relationship they'd like to develop. These include "I love you" romance rituals, weekly family meetings, yearly family growth retreats, special coming-of-age milestones for their children, holiday traditions, and a Yearly Meaning Snapshot.

The Story of Us Book. This is the visual representation of Allison and Jason's family Meaning Legacy Plan. It has a beautiful printout of their Coat of Arms, their principles, master stories (i.e., stories about their childhood memories, how they first met, their parents, the births of their children), heritage and family tree, and their Personal Legacy Statements.

Legacy Letters. Allison and Jason each write their own legacy letter for the family. This letter describes their love for their family, offers pieces of advice, and covers things they have learned. They then decide to write a letter to each child. These letters talk about the strengths of each child, specific advice, and the specific reasons their parents love them so dearly. The letters are stored on their family website as well as printed and stored in a small safe at the family's home. Allison and Jason will review these letters and update them yearly. Although their three-year-old doesn't understand the concept and their seven-year-old is not quite there yet either, their nine-year-old lights up with pride when Allison reads her letter praising her. They decide they will give a legacy letter to each child at specific milestones—when they learn how to drive, at graduation, when they get married or engaged, at the birth of a first child, and so on.

Family Brain Trust. We help the family set up an online brain trust and plan their first structured learning experience. They decide as a family that they are going to build a small boat together and learn about craftsmanship, and then document it on their family website and commemorate the entire experience with a trip to the lake in their new boat once it's complete.

Family Story Time. Allison and Jason want their children to know family stories. So they trade off telling their children a family story every night. They audio-record these stories and archive them on their family website. At the end of each year, they compile a book of their favorite stories.

Giving Day. Once a month, a member of the family gets to decide how he or she would like the family to spend a day of giving. This is a concept Allison and Jason came up with to involve their family in philanthropic work. In May, their nine-year-old daughter decided to spend a Saturday helping a local animal shelter with an animal fair it put on in the park to try to find homes for cats and dogs. In June, Jason wanted to participate in a walk for cancer. So the family all walked together and got their neighbors involved. In July, their three-year-old (with the help of some brainstorming from his mom) decided the family should make cookies for everyone in their neighborhood and take them around and meet the neighbors. Each project is documented—along with pictures and the occasional video—on the family's website.

Yearly Meaning Snapshot. Allison and Jason wish to create a Yearly Meaning Snapshot for themselves—one for Allison and one for Jason—and for their children. They plan to do this every December, at the close of each year. Over time, they will have two pages that represent each family member's life for that year.

File Storing and Sharing. We create a place for Allison and Jason to store their most important files and set up a family website that the family can use to share stories, ideas, and memories.

Parents with Young Kids
Case Study

Objectives

1. To create solid principles and guidelines to increase love, loyalty, and peace within our home.

2. To make time for our relationship and personal growth.

3. To create a family brand that represents love.

4. To create systems within the home to decrease the amount of chaos and increase our children's responsibility.

5. To prepare our children to become independent people who have high self-esteem, gratitude, a sense of responsibility, passion, and competence, and who are ready to leave the nest when they are old enough.

Results

Meaning Legacy™ Plan

Detailing goals, values, principles, and ways Allison and Jason would like to raise their children and implement their legacy.

First Family Meeting

Meet with the whole family and begin to construct the family mission, mantra, family rules, and values with the children.

Coat of Arms

Representative of the family's principles. Printed on archival paper, then framed and displayed at their home

Rituals & Traditions

A plan of weekly, monthly and yearly traditions, including weekly family meetings, Yearly Meaning Snapshot, etc.

Stories of Us Book™

Includes the coat of arms, their principles, master stories, heritage and family tree, and their mission, mantra and rules.

Legacy Letters

Allison and Jason each write their own legacy letter for the family and one for each child.

Family Brain Trust

The family plans their first structured learning experience and document what they learn on their family website (online family brain trust).

Family Story Time

Allison and Jason tell family stories to their children every night and record the best ones, then archive them on their family website.

Giving Day

Once a month, a member of the family gets to decide how he or she would like the family to spend a day of giving.

Yearly Meaning Snapshot™

Two-page spread for each member of Allison and Jason's family that outlines their accomplishments, and their most important stories, lessons and joys over the last year.

File Storing and Sharing

A place for Allison and Jason to store their most important files and a website where the family can use to share stories, ideas, and memories.

15

Grandparents
Case Study

Situation

Leslie and Roy are in their late seventies and have four children and nine grandchildren, ranging from ages seven to twenty-two. Leslie and Roy are retired—sort of. Roy is still involved in projects at the business he started, although his son (in his fifties) acts as the CEO and now has more control over the family business. Leslie spends her time with friends, working with charities, writing, and helping with the grandkids. Both Leslie and Roy enjoy several vacations a year and try to stay close with their family.

"Family is a priority for us," says Leslie. "We want our grandkids to grow up well and know how much we love them."

"We tried to raise our children right," Roy says, "and they are doing a pretty good job raising their own kids. Kids are unpredictable, though. Did you know our granddaughter just dropped out of law school and announced she wants to move to New York and become a purse designer?" Roy shakes his head.

"Now, honey." Leslie rolls her eyes. "Jessica's a very good girl. She's so smart and talented. It's good she feels she can live the life she wants."

Roy sighs. "A purse designer? Becoming an attorney is a far better choice. I already had a job lined up for her at a top law firm in Boston. In my day, my parents would've disowned me."

"Good thing we're not in your day!"

"Anyway," Roy says, "we're here because we want to leave more than just money behind for our family. We want the family legacy to carry on and for our kids to make responsible choices with the money we do leave."

"Also," Leslie says, "we want to use some of our resources to create a closer family and have memorable experiences."

Objectives

In an initial Meaning Legacy planning meeting, Leslie and Roy outline the following objectives:

1. To create more meaningful moments with our children and grandchildren.

2. To stay engaged in life, feel alive, and feel like we have purpose.

3. To document our lives and our family heritage.

4. To help prepare our family to inherit financial assets and use them wisely.

5. To support the next generations in becoming independent people who have high self-esteem, gratitude, a sense of responsibility, passion, and competence.

Strategy

Our team spends a day with Leslie and Roy discussing their vision and gathering crucial information to construct their Meaning Legacy Plan. From there, we plan several meeting times to go through each step of the process and develop their creative content. After this content is complete, we plan a schedule for continued yearly legacy check-ins.

Outcome

Comprehensive Family Meaning Legacy Plan. The purpose of this plan is to outline the objectives of Leslie and Roy's legacy. It also provides specific instructions for implementation and lists immediate and long-term milestones.

Couple's Mission. Both Leslie and Roy want to continue into old age feeling vibrant, engaged, and like they have purpose. Defining themselves only in their parental or grandparent roles takes away from their depth as individuals and could cause their relationship with each other to suffer. It's important that they work on projects together and define what's important to them as a couple—including goals, activities, and rituals that bring them closer together. So, they create a mission that encompasses what is important to them at this stage of their lives.

Personal Legacy Statement Evaluation and Purpose-Driven Goals. When kids are at home and life is busy with work, it's difficult to focus on personal development. As Leslie and Roy experience more free time, there is more opportunity to consider how they could develop themselves and switch their focus to using a lifetime of skills and wisdom to help others through mentoring or other means. They define a handful of personal goals and ways they'd like to contribute to their own growth and helping others in the coming years.

Rituals and Traditions. We work with Leslie and Roy to document traditions of the past and determine if new traditions make sense for the family. They are careful not to overstep, as they understand that it is their children's role to parent their own children. But they do want to continue some traditions that they establish, such as holidays, Sunday dinners, special vacations, and more.

Wisdom Memoir. Because Leslie loves to write, she will write a book entitled *Admirable Traits and Family Quirks* that will talk about relatives and their personal philosophies mixed with their funny quirks (e.g., Uncle Jimmy's strange habit of humming the national anthem in church, and Aunt Gladys's insistent honesty that resulted in her walking five miles in the snow to return incorrect change a store clerk had given her). After this memoir, Leslie is thinking of writing another book about the grandchildren as seen through the eyes of their pets.

Legacy Letters. Leslie and Roy write a letter to each of their children. They decide to give them to their children now rather than waiting. Their daughter cries and finally forgives them for an unfortunate event that happened in the past. Their son opens up more about his feelings. The other two children express their love and gratitude. Leslie and Roy then write letters to each grandchild. Each letter is then stored on a family website and in a safe deposit box.

Family Heritage. Leslie and Roy prioritize researching their family heritage. Our illustrators create a beautiful family tree for them, and they have a copy printed up for each of their children to hang in their homes. They also add favorite family stories to their website and give access to their kids and grandkids.

Video Series. Leslie and Roy hire a videographer to film them and different family members talking about memories and stories. These videos are put on the family website, and a final video is edited together and then sent out to each of their kids.

Family Retreat. Leslie, Roy, and their kids plan a family retreat in which they focus on having fun, plus some educational components. They have a "money day," where Roy talks about all that goes into managing the business and family assets.

Buying Trips. Leslie decides to take the grandkids on what she calls "buying trips," where the kids have a couple hours to go window shopping at the mall, come back to their grandmother, and tell her what they'd like to spend $50 on and why. Then they can buy that item. This helps the kids become analytical, less impulsive, and think about how to save or spend limited resources. Plus, it's a fun time with Grandma.

Mentoring Days. Because Roy and Leslie are concerned about their kids and grandkids being responsible with their inheritance, they set up days in which they can pair up family members with their financial advisors, money managers, and estate attorneys. Leslie and Roy think through the items their children/grandchildren need to master in the money arena and create a step-by-step mentorship program to help them. They store important educational resources online in their Family Brain Trust.

Yearly Meaning Snapshot. As in the previous case studies, Leslie and Roy see the value of capturing the most important highlights of their time spent with family each year and having it in a visual format to include as a part of a book or online post.

File Storing and Sharing. We create place for Roy and Leslie's family to store their most important files and set up a family website that they can use to share stories, ideas, and memories.

Grandparents
Case Study

Objectives

1. To create more meaningful moments with our children and grandchildren.

2. To stay engaged in life, feel alive, and feel like we have purpose.

3. To document our lives and our family heritage.

4. To help prepare our family to inherit financial assets and use them wisely.

5. To support the next generations in becoming independent people who have high self-esteem, gratitude, a sense of responsibility, passion, and competence.

Results

Meaning Legacy™ Plan

Detailing the objectives of Leslie and Roy's legacy and how they will implement each component.

Couple's Mission & Personal Legacy Statements

Outlining how Leslie and Roy want to continue into old age feeling vibrant, engaged, and like they have purpose.

Rituals & Traditions

A plan of weekly, monthly and yearly traditions, including Sunday dinners and special vacations.

Wisdom Memoir™

Because Leslie loves to write, she plans to write a book entitled *Admirable Traits and Family Quirks*.

Legacy Letters

Leslie and Roy write a letter to each of their children.

Family Heritage

Leslie and Roy research their history, have an illustration of their family tree created, and archive their family stories online.

Video Series

A videographer to films family members talking about memories and stories. These videos are put on the family website.

Family Retreat

Leslie, Roy, and their kids plan a family retreat in which they focus on having fun, plus some educational components.

Buying Trips

Leslie takes the grandkids on "buying trips," which helps them become more analytical, less impulsive, and think about how to save or spend limited resources.

Mentoring Days

Leslie and Roy pair up family members with their financial advisors, money managers, and estate attorneys to teach them about managing the family's wealth.

Yearly Meaning Snapshot™

Two-page spread for each member of Leslie and Roy's family that outlines their accomplishments, and their most important stories, lessons and joys over the last year.

File Storing and Sharing

A place for Leslie and Roy to store their most important files and a website where the family can use to share stories, ideas, and memories.

16

Philanthropic Visionary
Case Study

Situation

Dave is a successful CEO and founder of an organic farm in California and wants to ramp up his giving efforts. "Each year, my farm gives 10 percent of our harvest to homeless food initiatives," he says. "We also give money to local charities to fight against labor trafficking, but I want to do more. I want to create bigger change." He smiles. "There are many independent farms all over the United States. I want to create a campaign to encourage them to give to the homeless in their communities, much like we've been doing all these years."

He holds up a picture of himself wearing a t-shirt with the logo of his new charity project. "I can be the spokesperson—unless, of course, we can get Taylor Swift to do it." He laughs. "I want to travel to these farms and communities, and try to make a difference."

Objectives

In an initial Meaning Legacy planning meeting, Dave outlines the following objectives:

1. To spread his message throughout the United States, one farm at a time.

2. To recruit supporters in each farming community.

3. To document his journey and have the stories of those his organization has helped featured in social media.

Strategy

Our team spends a day with Dave outlining his vision and gathering crucial information to construct a public Meaning Legacy Plan. From there, we plan several meeting times to go through each step of the process and develop campaigns, creative content, and an action plan.

Outcome

Comprehensive Public Meaning Legacy Plan. The purpose of this plan is to outline the goals and vision Dave has for his philanthropic work. This includes what kind of message he'd like to publicly release, his content strategy for social media and outreach to other farms, and planning what collateral pieces need to be developed.

Collateral Pieces. Our team creates a website, brochure, direct mail pieces and other items to spread Dave's idea.

Internal Branding. There will be people who really get behind Dave's idea and support him. A part of the plan we develop is determining how he's going to recognize them and make them a part of his legacy vision so that it becomes a joint vision and they have a sense of ownership. This is done through messaging, sharing stories, special events, highlighting supporters for their role, and more.

Stories of Love Book. Dave's organization decides to release a book every year of the best stories and pictures from the service each community provides.

The Creation of a Legend. We create a PR campaign that focuses on the good works of the organization. Some of the "publicity" is our own doing, such as creating beautiful blog posts, social media content, and emails that we send to a list of supporters. Other publicity is the result of contacting appropriate media channels, which feature stories about Dave and his organization.

Philanthropic Visionary
Case Study

Objectives

1. To spread his message throughout the United States, one farm at a time.

2. To recruit supporters in each farming community.

3. To document his journey and have the stories of those his organization has helped featured in social media.

Results

Meaning Legacy™ Plan

Outlining the goals and vision Dave has for his philanthropic work. This includes what kind of message he'd like to publicly release, his content strategy, and planning what collateral pieces need to be developed.

Collateral Pieces

A website, brochure, direct mail pieces and other items to spread Dave's idea.

Internal Branding

To involve people in Dave's vision and make it a joint vision. This is done through messaging, sharing stories, special events, highlighting supporters, and more.

Stories of Love Book

Dave's organization releases a book every year of the best stories and pictures from the service each community provides.

Creation of a Legend

PR campaign that focuses on the good works of the organization, including blog posts, social media content, emails, articles, interviews, news stories, and so on.

Ready to Plan Your Legacy?

Meaning Legacy Resources

We have a variety of additional resources for you to access at **www.meaninglegacytools.com**. On this website, you'll find:

- Meaning Legacy assessment and checklist

- Family legacy planning recommendations (how to create a coat of arms, design an effective Brain Trust website, collect family stories, etc.)

- Links to educational content and articles

Subscription to *Legacy Arts*

For a free subscription to our online magazine, visit **www.legacyartsmagazine.com**. In every issue, we interview fascinating people about their legacies—from Fortune 500 CEOs to artists to philanthropic leaders to bestselling authors. We also offer tips, guidance, and strategies for developing an excellent legacy of your own.

Acknowledgements

The author gratefully acknowledges the help and efforts of several people for the writing of this book.

Thank you to all those who I've interviewed or have written articles about legacy development and non-financial success for *Legacy Arts* magazine. There are far too many to list by name, but I have found that this publication has attracted some of the most amazing people I have ever had the pleasure of speaking with; I've learned more from them than from any other source about how to become an exceptional human being. Much of their wisdom and advice inspired topics in this book.

Our team for the magazine is the best I've worked with. Content Director William Jenkins, in particular, has been an invaluable addition to the team and has made the magazine shine. Designer Marko Nedeljkovic has been there since the beginning and makes every article an artwork of its own.

Thank you to the wealth managers, financial advisors, and estate planning attorneys who spent time with me discussing their views on legacy and how it relates to financial structuring and generational wealth transfer. And to clients, friends, team members, and colleagues who each have offered their unique perspectives.

A special shout out to the Carlsbad EOT writing group that comprises several gifted writers who have each taught me so much about compelling writing, sentence structure, and story arc. Plus, they throw some fantastic parties. I'm so grateful to call them my friends.

Thank you to Jenna Rohrbacher for her excellent editing skills as well as the many people who gave feedback and helped with the conceptualization of the supplemental educational materials and website.

I'm incredibly fortunate to have had grandparents who made it a priority to keep our family connected and to maintain traditions as a part of our family legacy. My parents have always been supportive of my endeavors and I'm so grateful to them. My siblings are amazing people and I consider them some of my closest friends. Even though my family is far from perfect, there are components of our joint legacy that serve as the foundation for my work.

Lastly, thank you, Jeff Hill, for being the man I look forward to building my legacy with.